Richard Roberts has written a great book on prophecy, *Redeeming Prophecy: A Practical Guide to Authentic Prophetic Ministry*. He looks at prophecy through the lens of biblical, historical, and contemporary models. I found it helpful, practical, and an easy quick read of only about 150 pages. There are current issues related to prophecy that makes it very timely. Dr Roberts brings his insights as a medical doctor, a congregational leader, a psychotherapist, and one who has received training in the prophetic. He lays out whether or not a model for the prophetic has a consistent basis in scripture and church history.

The latter part of the book looks at some of the primary issues involved in our time. He deals with what prophecy is, how it is received, the different ways it can be received, whether it is happening today, its unique role in scripture and the life of the Church, the importance of creating a culture for prophecy and protocols for prophecy, the importance of weighing or judging it, and how prophecy involves revelation. I found his comments on 'revelation' today for the Church and its members to be very helpful. Dr Roberts includes words of knowledge and words of wisdom, as other revelatory gifts that are also prophetic.

He deals with the 'hot topics' related to prophecy today, such as the idea that prophets are strategists, and after the biblical and historical tests finds this belief having little support. The second 'hot topic' is the relationship between prophecy and politics. This section is of great interest, and I think has important insights pointing out mistakes of the recent past. I recommend *Redeeming Prophecy* for anyone wanting to learn more about prophecy and who desires to prophesy.

**Dr Randy Clark**, *Overseer of the apostolic network of Global Awakening*

I believe Richard Roberts's book, *Redeeming Prophecy*, is an extremely important contribution to the role which prophets and prophecy play, placing this subject as core in the development of our personal lives and the life of our churches today. It comes at a time when many Charismatic, and possibly some Pentecostal Churches, have allowed the gift to slip out of use while, on the other hand, in these worrying times, many saints are hanging on every word which emerges from the numerous 'celebrity prophets' who have appeared on the Internet over recent years. Richard does not offer his work as having all the answers but as a refreshingly helpful and biblical resource to all who would seek the Holy Spirit for more of his power in their lives and churches.

**John Noble**, *Chair of the UK Charismatic Leaders Conference (1984-2006)*

Spiritual gifts are powerful expressions of God's Spirit given to us, not only for our own personal benefit but also for the benefit of others. The Apostle Paul was clear when he said, *'I hope and pray that all would move in the gift of prophecy'*. This makes sense when we understand that true prophecy aims to build up, edify, bring comfort and exhortation. In other words, when people in the Church are building each other up, this creates a powerful community.

Prophecy is often one of the most misunderstood spiritual gifts, least pastored, and as with any spiritual gift, if not grounded in and through the lens of scripture, can create confusion and damage. Spiritual gifts are powerful tools distributed by the Spirit of God in order for the Church to operate in the power we've been called to live from. However, as with any power, when misdirected or misused, it can cause harm. As the recipient of the gift of prophecy, I have also seen the damage created when it operates for personal agenda, rather than to build up, encourage, edify or bring comfort.

We need helpful guides alongside the scriptures to help us, not only to be equipped to receive prophecy but also to move in the gift itself. Richard's book offers helpful insights addressing some of the very issues and concerns we have seen arise in the Church these last several years. If you want to explore the gift of prophecy, then I recommend Richard's book as one of the guides on your journey towards deeper understanding, and towards appreciating the various layers of prophetic ministry.

**Christy Wimber**, *Author, Former head pastor, International Speaker, Director of Global Church Planting, Friends Churches*

I like Richard Roberts's approach of bringing the ministry of prophecy back into balance among Christians. Catholic and Orthodox readers will find very interesting parallels between weighing prophecy and the discernment process used by the Vatican and other hierarchical bodies to authenticate visions and mystical experiences.

The 'celebrity prophet' concept adds to the cult of personality infecting society and the Church. I am convinced that most biblical prophecies started as being personal in nature as opposed to being corporate, but that they took on universal authority, and were given by people who were reluctant prophets! Even the prophecy foretelling the Virgin birth at the incarnation was a personal call to Ahaz to seek a sign. It had global implications and timeless application. That is the benefit of authentic prophecy in the Body of Christ. It is outside of time yet spans all time. Prophecy helps Christians internalise the Word of God as a Person, makes us His real presence and helps us fulfil Jesus's ministry as Priest, Prophet and King.

**Deacon Darrell Wentworth**, *Awakening the Domestic Church, Executive Producer CMAX TV*

Richard's book is an insightful and timely thought-provoker for anyone who appreciates the benefits of prophetic ministry. He draws on personal and professional experience to bring a rich breadth of insights that I am sure will benefit individuals and congregations.

**Clive Orchard**, *Warden, Ffald y Brenin Retreat Centre, Wales*

The prophetic movement has exploded on the radar of many Christians in recent church history and with it a good deal of tension as well as blessing to the larger Body of Christ. Richard's new book, *Redeeming Prophecy: A Practical Guide to Authentic Prophetic Ministry,* is a welcome addition to a current issue which needs some timely wisdom in prophetic protocol. Richard's book is not as much a 'how to' manual, but rather, a deep dive into the nature and function of the prophetic. After reading the book, you will have a greater appreciation not only for the gift of prophecy but for the entire Christian faith; and I believe will want to pursue the prophetic with renewed zeal. Great job, Richard!

**Dr Scott T. Kelso**, *Chairman, Charismatic Leaders Fellowship and author of Theological Violence in the 21$^{st}$ Century*

# Redeeming Prophecy

Previously published as
*We See in Part:
Reframing Prophecy Today*

# Redeeming Prophecy

## A Practical Guide to Authentic Prophetic Ministry

RICHARD J ROBERTS

Finnian Press

Copyright © 2023 Richard J Roberts

Previously published as © We See in Part: Reframing Prophecy Today (2023).

All rights reserved. This book or any portion thereof may not be reproduced or used in any manner whatsoever without the express written permission of the author except for the use of brief quotations in a book review.

Unless otherwise indicated, all Scripture quotations are from The Holy Bible, English Standard Version® (ESV®), copyright © 2001 by Crossway, a publishing ministry of Good News Publishers. Used by permission. All rights reserved.

Print ISBN    978-1-8384190-6-6
Digital ISBN  978-1-8384190-5-9

The Finnian Press
36 Culverhayes
Beaminster
DT8 3DG
UK

# Contents

| | |
|---|---:|
| ACKNOWLEDGEMENTS | 3 |
| INTRODUCTION | 5 |
| WHAT IS PROPHECY? | 13 |
| RECEIVING REVELATION | 22 |
| PROPHECY IN DIFFERENT GUISES | 31 |
| IS PROPHECY OPERATIVE TODAY? | 40 |
| THE UNIQUE ROLE OF PROPHECY | 49 |
| THE WHO & HOW OF PROPHECY | 55 |
| REVEALED KNOWLEDGE | 63 |
| A WORD OF WISDOM | 70 |
| DREAMS & VISIONS | 79 |
| CREATING A CULTURE FOR PROPHECY | 86 |
| DEVELOPING A PROTOCOL FOR PROPHECY | 92 |
| WEIGHING PROPHECY | 101 |
| PROPHECY, INTUITIONS & HUNCHES | 111 |
| GROWING IN PROPHECY | 120 |
| REFRAMING PROPHECY TODAY | 131 |
| FINAL THOUGHTS | 140 |
| FURTHER READING | 147 |
| ABOUT THE AUTHOR | 151 |

# Acknowledgements

Many people have helped, directly and indirectly, in the creation of this book. First and foremost, my wife, Norma, has worked tirelessly to edit both the grammar and the content of this work, making many helpful suggestions along the way. She provided several of the quotations, and her photograph of the Marshwood Vale in Dorset was used for the cover of the book and was the inspiration for the title.

My thanks and much appreciation also go to Simon Roberts who designed the cover (www.simonroberts.co.uk).

Several friends reviewed or made comments on the manuscript, including David Lawrence, whose advice and comments have been most helpful. I am also very grateful to Malcolm Dunn who edited the final manuscript.

Thanks is due to my friend Robb Sykes, who, following conversations at his home in Orangeville, Ontario, encouraged me to write something on the topic of prophecy. I am also indebted to those who gave permission for their stories to be included in this book.

I would like to thank my church family at The Meeting Place, particularly those with whom I regularly pray and whose support and, at times, prophetic input has encouraged me along the way.

# Introduction

## The Need to Test All Things

> Do not quench the Spirit. Do not despise prophecies, but test everything; hold fast what is good.
> 1 THESSALONIANS 5:19-21

There are an estimated 600 million Charismatic and Pentecostal Christians in the world.[1] This is approximately a quarter of the whole Church, representing an astonishing 8% of the world's population. This means that 1 in 13 people accept the validity of spiritual gifts, including prophecy. That's a lot of prophecy!

There is much variety in the way in which prophecy is exercised and delivered in different settings. There may, for example, be someone in a prayer group using everyday language to describe to others 'a picture' which has formed in their mind's eye. Elsewhere there may be someone standing up in a congregation declaring 'thus saith the Lord...' Prophecy operates in a wide spectrum of contexts, ranging from the sharing of revelation in a small home group to the pronouncements of those who are, in effect, celebrity prophets and whose predictions may gain hundreds of thousands of internet hits.

In some settings, those who regularly exercise prophetic gifts are attributed with considerable authority by their hearers. This is the case

---

[1] The figure of 600 million Charismatic/Pentecostals is a conservative estimate and Peter Hocken suggests that there are almost 400 million Charismatics within the historic churches alone (*The Challenges of the Pentecostal, Charismatic & Jewish Messianic Movements*).

in several large African churches and movements where their founders are regarded as prophets - such as the powerful West African evangelist and church planter William Wade Harris. Similarly, some regions in the West now have what has been termed 'councils of prophets' who use the internet to share what they believe to be the word of the Lord for their locality or their country and whose views are highly regarded by many. The charismatic landscape is certainly diverse.[2]

What should we make of this diverse, and at times confusing, picture? Are all these forms of prophecy legitimate or are some aspects suspect, or even risky? We need some guidelines to help us discern so that we can 'hold fast what is good' – and by implication let go of what is not so good.

Despite this diversity and, at times, confusion, the apostolic injunction to 'not despise prophecies' is clear. Underpinning this book is the conviction that prophecy, fresh revelation for today, remains an essential component of church life. It was of utmost importance for the early church, and even though there have been long periods when 'the word of the Lord was rare' (1 Samuel 3:1), prophecy has continued to play a vital role throughout the history of the Church.

## The Priority of the Activity of the Spirit

At times, we in the West have been tempted to replace prophecy with planning. We do see evidence of planning in the life of the early church, usually to deal with specific practical issues. For example, the apostles proposed a plan to delegate food distribution to widows to 'seven men of good reputation, full of the Spirit and wisdom', while they devoted themselves to prayer and preaching. This proposal met with approval and had excellent results (Acts 6:1-7). Similarly, there was a sound strategy behind Paul's missionary journeys which tended to follow a logical pattern, utilising major trade routes. But even so, it

---

[2] 'Charismatic' can have various meanings. The Charismatic Movement is a term which embraces Christians who are not Pentecostal but practise the gifts of the Spirit, whether in denominational or non-denominational churches. The term 'Charismatic' also has a broader meaning and can include both Pentecostals and those in the Charismatic Movement.

was the voice of the Spirit that launched Paul and Barnabus on their first missionary journey (Acts 13:1-3). And on several occasions, we see the action of the Holy Spirit superseding Paul's original plans:

> And they went through the region of Phrygia and Galatia, having been forbidden by the Holy Spirit to speak the word in Asia. And when they had come to Mysia, they attempted to go into Bithynia, but the Spirit of Jesus did not allow them. And a vision appeared to Paul in the night, a man of Macedonia... immediately, we sought to go into Macedonia.
> ACTS 16:6-10

It was also the Spirit who engineered the first revival on the Day of Pentecost (Acts 2). The disciples had to wait and pray, rather than come up with a cunning plan. (An interesting mental exercise is to think how we might have approached the situation they found themselves in. Would we have created a plan for the spread of the gospel, or would we have trusted the Holy Spirit and had the patience to wait?) Perhaps our need today, despite our ability to come up with strategies, is to renew our dependency on the Holy Spirit – the Spirit of prophecy.[3]

## Misguided Prophecies

Many Christians today are rightly concerned about prophecy. Some believe it is misguided, or even quite dangerous.[4] Indeed, many of us have had first-hand experiences of the misuse of prophecy or poor prophetic practice, while some have even witnessed the abuse of prophetic gifts for personal gain. Concern has deepened in recent times because of several well-publicised political 'prophecies' in which events predicted failed to materialise.

These misguided prophetic words have now gained notoriety in the

---

[3] Pentecost is not an example of prophecy but it demonstrated the need for reliance on the Spirit of God.
[4] John F MacArthur is an example of someone who considers Charismatics to be guilty of gross error, whereas Jim Packer has been more moderate in his critique. See https://www.samstorms.org/enjoying-god-blog/post/not-all-cessationists-are-of-macarthurs-spirit

secular, as well as in the Christian, press.[5] Jeremiah Johnson, a well-known figure in the USA, apologised when his prophecies concerning the outcome of the 2020 election proved to be incorrect.[6] Although several of those involved have followed his example and publicly admitted their failings, others have refused to apologise and to learn lessons from their mistakes. Some have even used spurious theological arguments to bolster their position, discrediting further the legitimacy of contemporary prophecy. One common response has been to 'move the goalposts' and state that the prophecies were true in substance but that the date was wrong.[7] Yet the thrust of the majority of these prophecies was that they referred *specifically* to 2020, not to some later date.

Instances of the misuse of spiritual gifts have led many to turn their back altogether on the charismatic dimension of the Christian life. I recently talked with a couple who embrace a wide range of approaches to Christian spirituality in their walk with God. They are comfortable with the evangelical emphasis on the importance of scripture, the contemplative emphasis on silence and prayer and an activist approach to social justice. They are much less comfortable with charismatic practices, having witnessed various excesses.

There are four major areas which we need to address if people are to be saved not only from being permanently disillusioned but also from being separated from prophecy's influence in their lives:

- We need to reaffirm the central place that prophecy should play in the life of the people of God.

- We need to understand the full spectrum of prophetic gifts.

- We need to ensure that adequate safeguards are in place.

---

[5] I will refer to any communication that purports to be from God as a 'prophecy' including both the false and the genuine ends of the prophetic continuum. For examples of controversial prophecies and their effect on voters see: https://www.politico.com/news/magazine/2021/02/18/how-christian-prophets-give-credence-to-trumps-election-fantasies-469598
[6] https://www.christianitytoday.com/ct/2021/july-august/trump-prophets-election-jeremiah-johnson-reckoning-charisma.html
[7] For an example of this see https://www.newsweek.com/christian-prophets-who-predicted-donald-trumps-reinstatement-2021-no-apologies-1665157

- We need to look again at the witness and teaching of scripture, our measuring stick, so that we can 'test all things'.

## Rethinking Prophecy

Many helpful books have been penned on the topic of prophecy. Well-known authors include Mike Bickle, Jack Deere, Graham Cooke, Randy Clark (Independent Charismatic), Mike Breen, David Pytches (Anglican), Bruce Yocum, Charles Whitehead, and John Michael Talbot (Catholic). Most of these books outline basic practices, such as how to prophesy and how to test prophecy.[8]

Despite the excellent advice contained in these books, very few of them address the knottier issues that many are asking about today - the recently published *Prophetic Integrity* by R T Kendall being an exception. Kendall affirms the value of contemporary prophecy citing several positive examples from his own experience. He then evaluates the failed 'political prophecies' which circulated widely in the USA in the early 2020s. His critique is well-argued, and he certainly pulls no punches.

As well as the issue of false or misguided prophecy, several other important issues are rarely addressed. One such issue is the power dynamics that can come into play when prophetic words are delivered in controlling ways. There is also the possibility, rarely considered, that some 'prophecies' might simply be astute observations, rather than divine revelation. The fact that unchurched people frequently make accurate observations and have intuitions might also make us reconsider which factors are unique to Christian prophecy.

These sorts of questions need careful consideration and require credible answers. Prophecy is widely exercised and has a broad scope and contemporary practice should be addressed honestly and comprehensively. This is important both for the vitality and health of the Church itself and for the standing of the Church in the world so that we might be prepared to give a defence for our faith when challenged. The following questions draw from issues raised in this book:

---

[8] The details of all books mentioned in this work can be found in the Further Reading section.

- What is the unique role of prophecy compared to that of scripture?
- Can we survive or thrive without prophecy?
- Is prophecy optional, an added extra for keen Christians?
- How acceptable is it that some prominent prophetic voices expect to be trusted and taken very seriously, often without much scrutiny?
- How accurate should we expect contemporary prophecy to be?
- If prophecy is a mixture of divine and human elements, how can we differentiate between the two?
- How much weight should we put on a prophecy which indicates that a particular course of action be taken?

## Contemporary Practice & the Bible

The questions listed above come from the common experiences of many Christians, but questions also arise when some current day practices are compared with what is seen in the Bible. How much should we expect contemporary prophecy to conform to examples given in scripture? Can we endorse practices which, although they do not contravene scripture, have no biblical precedent? One example of a practice not seen in scripture is praying and prophesying over lines of people. This dates back to the 1940s and a movement which started in Canada known as The Latter Rain Movement. Those involved promoted the laying on of hands accompanied by prayer and prophecy to 'impart' blessing to people.

I recently contributed to a conference during which the host invited people to come forward for this form of prayer. I have limited experience in praying for lines of people and I usually check whether my prayers seem to be along the right lines. Despite people generally confirming that I am on the right lines, I usually feel anxious in these circumstances! This is partly related to concern as to whether people will weigh what I sense about them. I hope that they will not simply accept what is said because of being endorsed by the conference host.

Another cause of concern is related to what is found in the Bible. I am aware that scriptural examples of this sort of mass prayer usually involved a prominent figure praying, blessing, or prophesying over people whom they knew intimately. Jacob prayed for his offspring rather than for relative strangers (see Genesis 49 and also Deuteronomy 33). Any prophetic sense he had concerning the future of those prayed for was likely to have been formed over time, involving observation as well as revelation. So where does this leave me, praying for a line of people I barely know? It does not contravene scripture, but is it legitimate as there is no clear warrant in the Bible for this fairly common practice?

The Bible also provides another form of critique for contemporary practice. An in-depth study of the Old and New Testaments will reveal that we sometimes neglect certain prominent aspects of biblical prophecy. Many are comfortable with prophecy for upbuilding, encouragement and consolation (1 Corinthians 14:3) but are much less sure about directive or predictive prophecy, both of which we see in the Bible. Some in the contemporary Church underplay other features of prophetic ministry, such as the emphasis on social justice seen in many of the Old Testament prophets (as well as in the New Testament epistles, particularly in James). Few contemporary charismatic prophets seem to have embraced this as a major theme of their ministry.

Another often underemphasised aspect of biblical prophecy was highlighted as the centre of Christianity shifted to the global South in the last century. The Protestant missionary movement had exported a western understanding of Christianity to the developing world and mission was 'from the West to the rest' (of the world). But once the Bible was translated into local and regional languages, non-western readers observed features that were often overlooked in the West. African Christians live in a culture which is attuned to the supernatural and they noticed that prophetic revelation often comes via dreams. Those of us in the West might do well to take more seriously the words of Joel: 'Your young men shall see visions and your old men *dream dreams*'. In fact, a friend recently encouraged me to pay more attention to my own dreams.

Much of what follows is an attempt to critique our current practice of prophecy in the light of scripture. New practices will, at times, be legitimate responses to changing situations. But in biblical times when renewal occurred, scripture provided the framework to understand the fresh activity of the Holy Spirit. We see this in evidence when Peter used Joel's prophecy to explain Pentecost to his hearers: 'this is that *which was written...*' The events of Pentecost were not exactly what Joel had predicted but his prophecy acted as a frame through which otherwise inexplicable events were rendered intelligible. Hence, the use of scripture in this book is highlighted as a guide to, and interpreter of, contemporary prophecy.

## How to Use this Book

This book aims to provide a framework, using both practical and biblical perspectives, to inform the conversation around prophecy. It is intended to be a starting point to explore several questions relating to prophetic gifts. I hope that the concepts explored will be conversation starters, leading to reflection, dialogue and possibly change. Indeed, I am sure that, through an ongoing dialogue about this topic, my views will also be modified.

If you are interested in specific aspects of prophetic ministry – such as how to weigh prophecy or how to interpret the imagery present in dreams/visions - you might wish to be selective and read just the chapters on those topics. If, however, you wish to gain an overview of all aspects of prophecy I would encourage you to read this book in its entirety. Many of the themes touched upon initially are developed more fully in subsequent chapters and some issues which, at first sight, might seem less relevant may prove to be the most important.

I hope, however much or little is read, that you enjoy reading it and find it stimulating, even if you end up disagreeing with some of my conclusions!

# 1

# What is Prophecy?

This chapter aims to establish what is meant by prophecy, prophets, and prophetic ministry and is a foundation for the book as a whole. It identifies several key issues to be explored later, such as the nature of revelation and how prophecy is communicated and weighed. The discussion of other topics, such as the place of prophecy in the political arena or the way in which prophetic ministry can be used as a cover for narcissistic traits, is framed by our understanding of these foundational issues.

In order to address the question 'what is prophecy?' I start by describing some of the experiences which have shaped my own views. Among other things, my story illustrates some of the dangers inherent when prophecy is in operation, particularly when the place of prophetic gifts in the life of the Church is overvalued. My experiences give a context for my views.

## A Personal Journey

The exploration of prophecy began for me in my mid-20s. I was sitting in the lounge of my home reading the following passage of scripture:

> 'And he gave the apostles, the prophets, the evangelists, the shepherds and teachers… for building up the body of Christ…'
> EPHESIANS 4:11-12

I was vaguely aware that these different sorts of ministries had been given to the Church by the ascended Christ, but I was not terribly clear what they each represented. As I scanned the list, the term 'prophet' really stood out. I was intrigued, although I had no idea what a prophet might look like. I had never heard a talk or read a book on the subject. Thus it was, immersed in the Bible and captivated by these two verses, that I began a long journey of exploration.

Some years after this, I came across a church which emphasised the importance of prophetic ministry. I corresponded with the main leader of the church asking him to comment on my questions concerning prophecy, prophets and other topics of interest. Eventually, we ended up moving to the Southwest of England to join this church as I wanted to learn everything I could about prophecy but, tragically, almost from the start things went awry. The church became enamoured with its particular emphasis, pride crept in, and things went rapidly downhill. The church became more and more isolated from the wider Christian community and five years later it was disbanded altogether due to unresolved internal difficulties.

On the positive side, this was a church that took prophecy seriously. I read several popular and a number of academic books on prophecy, some by leading theologians. There was a strong focus on understanding the prophetic books of the Bible and, consequently, I devoured commentaries and books on the Revelation of John. I gained first-hand experience of the exercise of prophetic gifts and had the opportunity to discuss prophetic ministry with people who had thoroughly researched the topic in church history and who had also experienced it in practice. In short, I received a good grounding in the workings and use of prophecy. On the negative side, there was an overemphasis on the importance of prophecy with very little awareness of the need for other forms of ministry. In particular, the roles of pastoral and evangelistic ministry were poorly understood and were distorted and underemphasised respectively.

While I was made aware of the positive potential of prophecy, I observed some serious unintended consequences arising from prophecy being mishandled and saw for myself some of the pitfalls of prophetic ministry. At times, leaders were controlling, which is always a danger where there is the belief that leaders hear God for others, more clearly than the 'others' in question can themselves.

This experience overall heightened my awareness of the dangers of isolation and pride, especially when Christian leaders are highly gifted prophets. The importance of character was firmly underlined. I am convinced that in God's eyes, character, the fruit of the Spirit in our lives, is much more important than giftedness. The combination of great gifts and unchecked character flaws wreaks havoc, something which, sadly, I have also observed in other settings.

## Going Deeper

Shortly after the demise of this prophetically centred church, a new church began to develop from the house group of which we had been part. This development was 'accidental' rather than strategic as church leadership had not been part of my thinking. As a result, in the late 1980s, I ended up in a busy medical practice while leading this newly-formed church, a combination that was difficult to sustain. At this time, I was also aware that, despite all efforts, our former church setting had gone badly wrong, and that I needed to process this and make sense of it. These factors led me to consider a career change and I retrained to work part-time in psychotherapy. This not only released time for church, but also furnished me with ways to conceptualise a whole range of human dynamics, including those involved in churches.

In the late 1990s, I took the exploration of prophecy a step further and enrolled in a Master of Arts in Theological Studies. This was a wonderful learning opportunity and a chance to have my ideas tested by those with greater theological acumen than I possessed.

Although I had not planned to do so, I realised in retrospect that virtually all my chosen essay titles related to the topic of prophecy. My final dissertation also pursued this theme, focusing on the relationship between the ministry of Dr Martin Luther King Jr and the Biblical Prophets.

## The Nature of Prophecy

> The word of the Lord came to me: 'What do you see, Jeremiah?'
> JEREMIAH 1:11

God's question to Jeremiah, 'What do you see?', is crucial to an understanding of prophecy. Most Charismatic Christians would agree that prophecy in all its forms involves 'seeing' revelation from God. Revelation is the experience of a eureka moment when we see something clearly. In the UK we use the phrase 'the penny has dropped' to describe the sudden realisation which comes when, having wrestled with our confusion, we exclaim, 'Oh, I see!'

By contrast the popular view of prophecy, as held by the man or woman in the street, is that it is a form of clairvoyance, usually associated with religion or other spiritual practices. When the average person hears the word 'prophecy', he or she might think of Nostradamus, the French astrologer, popularly credited with accurately predicting the future. Or perhaps self-appointed prophets, such as Jim Jones, come to mind; people who might prey upon other people's religious convictions to lead them astray.

The term 'prophet' is sometimes used to describe astute political commentators, sociologists or even musicians such as Bob Dylan, because of the penetrating insights into the nature of contemporary society they may have. The nature of Christian prophecy is somewhat different from the ability to predict future events based on knowledge of psychology, history, politics, or sociology. I heard a talk in the 1990s in which a Christian social researcher predicted the coming New Age Movement. Although I thought he was somewhat deluded, his prediction proved accurate. His foresight was based on a solid understanding of social trends, but it was not prophecy in the biblical sense of the term.

A simple description of Christian prophecy might be that it consists of revelation being given to one person in order for it to be shared with another person or with a group of people. A prophecy intended for one individual is often referred to as *personal prophecy*. In contrast, if we receive revelation for ourselves, we usually refer to this as guidance, rather than prophecy.

## 'Prophecy' Has a Range of Meanings

Despite the simplicity of this description, the task of gaining a more nuanced understanding of the nature of Christian prophecy is complex because terms such as 'prophecy' are used in scripture without great precision. Words in any language, such as Hebrew and Greek, have a range of meanings which is determined by the context in which they are used. It is, therefore, important to appreciate that several different concepts are expressed under the umbrella term 'prophecy'.[9]

This is illustrated by considering the range of meanings of the word 'house'. House commonly refers to a dwelling place for human habitation and we know the difference between a house, a caravan, and a shack; caravans and shacks also being places of human habitation. And we are familiar with and understand the term 'greenhouse', allowing for the fact that greenhouses are neither homes nor are they coloured green. We appreciate that there is a core concept expressed by the term 'house' but that it has quite fuzzy edges and various shades of meaning (such as a place to house green vegetation). Yet despite often having blurred edges, words express a core meaning - we know what a dog is, even if there are hundreds of varieties, and we can easily distinguish dogs from cats. The term prophecy is the same, having a range of meanings but with a core concept.

## Prophetic Ministry

The term 'prophet', like prophecy, also has a range of meanings in the Bible. It is sometimes used simply to refer to someone who prophesies very occasionally. Samuel told Saul that he would meet a band of prophets and that the Spirit would fall upon him also. This was a life-transforming experience, but his calling was to be a king rather than to become a prophet. Nonetheless, the masses regarded him as having become a prophet through this dramatic experience and 'Is Saul also among the prophets?' became a popular saying (1 Samuel 10:5-13).

We see a similar use of the term prophet in Numbers 11. God told Moses that seventy elders would 'bear the burden of the people' alongside him and that this would happen once they had received the Spirit. Presumably, the Spirit would enable them to receive divine wisdom in carrying out their responsibilities, such as judging the complex issues people would bring to them. When the Spirit came on the elders, they prophesied, as a one-off occurrence (and this story

---

[9] The various meanings of a word are referred to as its *semantic range*. Semantic means 'meaning' and there is always a range of meanings for any word. This contrasts with the very precise use of terms we see in scientific or other technical publications.

affirms a strong link between receiving the Spirit and the gift of prophecy). Yet Moses regarded the seventy elders as having become prophets, even though prophecy did not continue to feature in their ministries:

> As soon as the Spirit rested on them, they prophesied. *But they did not continue doing it.*
> NUMBERS 11:25

Samuel and Elijah were also thought of as prophets, but in their case this referred to a life-long vocation. Prophetic ministry in the vocational sense usually involves a call from God which strengthens resolve, often in the face of conflict or opposition (*vocation* is derived from the Latin word *vocare*, which means 'to call'). Samuel and Elijah *regularly* prophesied and spoke words of knowledge and of wisdom. These different expressions of the concept of prophet demonstrate that we are dealing with a spectrum, with diversity and a variety of ways in which people function. At one end of the spectrum, there are prophets who occasionally prophesy – at the other end are those with a call to a particular sort of ministry.

Paul appears to use the term 'prophet' in both ways. In 1 Corinthians 14:29, it is likely that Paul was using 'prophets' to describe those who prophesied occasionally in a home-based church in Corinth (it is unlikely that a small home church would contain several people with a clear vocation to prophetic ministry). In other passages of scripture, the term 'prophet' described those with a clearly defined vocation. This involved church leadership in partnership with those exercising different ministries (1 Corinthians 12:29; Ephesians 3:4-5 & 4:11). For Paul, the term 'prophet' could indicate either end of this spectrum.

The phrase 'prophetic ministry' is commonly used today to describe the role of those clearly called to be prophets, although it is not a biblical term as such. Sometimes it is associated with the idea of the 'office of a prophet'. We should note that the word 'office', sometimes used in modern translations of the New Testament to refer to those who serve the Church, does not appear in the original Greek.[10]

---

[10] The word 'office' is inserted in some passages where elders, bishops and priests are mentioned. Those who defend its usage sometimes argue that every Christian has an office, not just leaders. This seems an unnatural – and

The concept of having an office is, however, firmly fixed in the minds of many theologians and church leaders.

The difficulty with using this term is that the Church is primarily a relational entity, whereas 'office' suggests a more institutional mode of existence. This is unhelpful as it distracts from the familial language that pervades and dominates the New Testament epistles. Office replaces ideas of kinship with an organisational framework (we wouldn't speak of the office of a mother or father!) It is a hierarchical and power-laden concept which detracts from the idea of ministry as service within the context of relationship. There are, therefore, several reasons why the term 'prophetic office' is best avoided.

## Prophetic Revelation

It is clear from the Bible that prophecy encompasses much variety under the core concept of the reception of receiving revelation. Prophetic revelation occurs when God shows us something that would otherwise be hidden from view. A link between prophecy and revelation is clearly seen in the stories of Samuel and Elisha. Their revelation was wide-ranging in its scope, addressing both mundane concerns, such as the whereabouts of Saul's missing donkeys, as well as matters of national importance, such as the fate of a king (1 Samuel 10:16; 2 Kings 8:10-14).

The Holy Spirit is the active force in genuine prophecy. This is evident in the way John prefaced his extended prophecy with the words, '*I was in the Spirit* on the Lord's Day...' (Revelation 1:10). It is revelation, imparted by the Spirit of God, which distinguishes prophecy from our own ideas, however profound, or from making an educated assessment of a situation.

Although revelation is the common denominator there are a variety of ways in which prophecy is received and the way in which God communicates with us varies from person to person. Joseph, for example, regularly received revelation in the form of a dream involving angels (Matthew 1:20; 2:13&19). Revelation may be received as words and phrases or as an image forming in our mind's

---

unnecessary - way to describe the concept that we each have a calling, gifts and ways in which we uniquely serve God and others.

eye; it can consist of revealed knowledge or divine wisdom. It can be in the form of a dream or vision or be more like a hunch or a strong inner conviction, concerning an individual or a group.

Prophecy may be received through a passage of scripture which God has impressed on someone and John Goldingay, professor of Old Testament at Fuller Theological Seminary, described how powerfully effective this can be. He and his wife were planning to move from a seminary in the UK to California to take up his teaching post although John had misgivings about this proposed course of action. One of his seminary students was sitting in chapel when she sensed God telling her to tell John that Judges 18:6 was God's promise to him.

Neither John nor the student could recall the verse in question but when they looked up Judges 18 it provided the reassurance that was needed to undertake the move to the USA: 'Go; do well. The journey on which you are going is under Yahweh's eye'. He believed that God was using this scripture to help him feel that their future was secure, despite the realisation that the reassurance given was unrelated to the original context of this verse. He felt it was particularly needed as his wife was disabled and the move was likely to have been challenging for them both.[11]

Whatever way God chooses to communicate with us we need, like the boy Samuel, to grow in our ability to discern the voice of God and to be able to differentiate God's voice from other voices (1 Samuel 3:1-9). It is, of course, easy to deceive ourselves that other voices, including our own, are the voice of God - it is of note that Samuel was guided in a discernment process by someone more experienced. Revelation can originate from spiritual sources other than God, and this also makes discernment of prophecy a priority, as we will discuss later.

Prophecy can be delivered in a variety of ways and in scripture we see not only words being used, but also, on occasions, the revelation being enacted in some way. Sometimes straightforward instructions were given and at other times prophets employed poetic language or told parables. In some instances, a prophetic revelation was quite detailed, but in other cases, it was more an outline of events. Highly

---

[11] Recounted in Goldingay J., *Joshua, Judges and Ruth for Everyone* (London, SPCK).

symbolic language might also be used, such as is seen in John's Revelation or in Zechariah's vision of a flying scroll.

It is crucial that we learn to distinguish between literal and symbolic representations of the future. Zachariah certainly warned of events to come, in particular of God's judgement, but few of his hearers would have expected to see an actual flying scroll (Zechariah 5:1-4). Failure to recognise the difference between literal and symbolic language can have disastrous consequences for the Church.[12]

It is possible that prophecy today may similarly be expressed in these different ways. It is also possible that it takes the form of song, contemporary poetry, various forms of art or through inspired preaching, although for some these may be more controversial suggestions. The next chapters will look in more detail at how we may receive and communicate prophetic revelation.

---

[12] Norman Cohn's book *The Pursuit of the Millennium* highlights the dangers of an overly literal interpretation of apocalyptic literature.

# 2

# Receiving Revelation

The previous chapter portrayed revelation as *the* defining feature of prophecy and prophetic ministry. In the New Testament, prophetic revelation is firmly and consistently linked with the activity of the Holy Spirit (e.g., in Acts 2, Acts 19:6 and Revelation 1:10). Receiving revelation is the first stage and prophecy is only complete when revelation is communicated *through us*, which involves using words and/or actions to convey what has been revealed. The hallmark of prophecy is this dynamic of revelation communicated *to us* and *through us*. The subject of this chapter is the first stage of prophecy – the actual reception of information, concepts, ideas, and images from God.

Revelation is, of course, key to many other aspects of Christian experience as well as to prophecy. It is a core component in discerning guidance, along with advice, common sense, and scripture. Perhaps most importantly, revelation is necessary for us to become personally convinced of the reality of God and of the Lordship of Jesus. The action of the Holy Spirit makes real to us what would otherwise simply be a doctrine.

The ways in which we receive revelation are the same whether we are considering a revelation of Jesus, personal guidance, prophecy, or conviction of sin (John 16:8-11). We can learn much about the dynamics of revelation by considering how it operates in all these aspects of Christian experience.

## Revelation Shapes our Lives & Ministries

The life of Paul helps us to appreciate the importance of revelation and how it might shape our present and our future. In Acts 9 we read an account of the conversion of Paul, who at that point was called Saul. He saw a light from heaven and heard the voice of Jesus saying, 'Saul, Saul, why are you persecuting me?' (Acts 9:4). Paul then asked a question, demonstrating that revelation may emerge from a direct dialogue with God. On asking who was speaking to him, he was informed, 'I am Jesus, whom you are persecuting'. This was a great shock for Paul, who up to that point believed that he was doing God's will by persecuting the Church. It was an immediate and life-changing revelation that had come in an instant but had a lasting effect. The experience may have formed the basis for a longer process of reflection which enabled him to receive further insight into the implications of his revelatory experience.

One thing that would have occurred to Paul was that he was not, in fact, persecuting Jesus, he was persecuting his followers. Perhaps Paul was introduced to the reality of the Church as Christ's body on earth by reflecting on the words of Jesus. He developed this theme when he wrote to the Corinthian church: 'Now you are the body of Christ and individually members of it' (1 Corinthians 12:27). My conjecture is that Paul's understanding of the nature of the Church, expressed in his letters to the Corinthians, emerged from reflecting on the Damascus Road experience. Further revelation on the meaning of this experience is likely to have given rise to his many sacrifices for the sake of the Church, which he closely identified with Jesus himself (his body).

Revelation may be received in an instant, but often it does its work slowly, as long as attention is given to it. Contemplation, which can be overlooked in more activist approaches to the Christian life, is the key to fully benefitting from revelation received. Revelation shaped Paul's life and ministry. Similarly, revelation shaped the ministry of his disciple, Timothy:

> 'This charge I entrust to you, Timothy, my child, *in accordance with the prophecies previously made about you,* that by them you may wage the good warfare...'
> 1 TIMOTHY 1:18

Revelation, in all its forms, is important: it shaped Paul's life, it shaped Timothy's life, and it can shape ours. What we have seen can shape what we become.

## Word & Event

Revelation is more than simply information. It can be crucial in releasing God's will in our lives due to its inherent creative potential. Prophecy in the Bible was sometimes introduced by the phrase 'the word of the Lord came to me'. Of course, the whole idea behind the reception of revelation is that the word of the Lord would eventually be spoken or written down, but first, it must be received, it must 'come to us'. One Hebrew term for 'word' is *dabar*, which is translated by the terms *logos* or *rhema* in the Greek version of the Old Testament (the Septuagint).

Dabar is usually translated as 'word', but it can also mean an event. This has given rise to a somewhat complex, and possibly esoteric, discussion concerning the relationship between God's word and events. Does God's word actually release the event that it declares, as is perhaps implied in the concept that it will not return void but will accomplish its purpose (Isaiah 55:11)? Often the word is effective in its own terms and creates the event of which it speaks, without depending on human cooperation. The prime example of the power of God's speech is found in early Genesis where Creation comes into existence purely by the command of God. The phrase 'by fiat', Latin for command, is used to describe this. Much biblical prophecy falls into the 'by fiat' camp.

In other instances, the event depends on our response to that word. An example of the link between word, response and event may be found in the words of Jesus to Peter that, although having caught nothing, he should cast his nets again. Peter's positive response ensured that the word became event (Luke 5:5-8).

## Receiving Revelation is a Subjective Experience

The reception of revelation is usually a subjective experience, except in those rare instances when someone hears the audible voice of God or of an angel. The word of God is communicated through human vessels, and, because of this, the final form of a prophetic word today will usually be the outcome of the synergy between God and the messenger. It may be more objective where specific words form in the mind of the prophet but in other instances, the prophet seems to use his or her own words to describe a visionary experience. This appears to be the case in Joel's prophecy, where he describes a prolonged vision of a plague of locusts, symbolising God's judgement on the people and the land.

Experience and scripture both suggest that God can communicate through impressions, an inner witness, or visions rather than through the impartation of clear and precise words and phrases. This means that the drainpipe model of prophecy, where we are simply dictating machines, frequently does not hold water (pun intended). A drainpipe receives water, and it passes through unchanged, whereas usually we are not simply passive recipients of God's word; often we must supply the words ourselves to give expression to what we sense in our spirit. This produces a somewhat complex situation for contemporary prophecy in that while the revelation received is accurate, *our words need weighing as we vary in our ability to accurately communicate or interpret what has been received.*

The subjective nature of prophecy can present a problem for those who, like me, were taught to rely on scripture and to discount our feelings. While I wholeheartedly concur with this sentiment in relation to the foundational issues of our faith, we see in scripture itself that experiential knowledge of God is highly valued (Psalm 34:8). An inner, subjective witness enabled two disciples to realise that they had encountered Jesus on the road to Emmaus: 'Did not our hearts *burn within us* as he talked with us on the road?' (Luke 24:32).

## The Experience of Revelation

There are a variety of ways in which people hear God and different people have different experiences as to how they receive revelation. Attempting to describe a subjective experience to another person is never easy unless the hearer herself has had a similar experience. Imagine trying to explain a particular piece of music to someone who has never heard it - even worse, if the person has no experience of music in any form. The best you could do would be to resort to analogies – 'It is a bit like this…' Conveying the nature of prophetic revelation is just as challenging as describing what music is like to a person who has never heard it. It is like trying to describe another language, another means of communication.

Prophetic revelation sometimes takes the form of a clear conviction that we are dealing with a God-idea, rather than a good idea. This may be accompanied by a high degree of certainty, or it may just be an inkling, a persistent feeling that we are on to something. We see an example of this in Paul's pastoral advice to the Corinthian church about the issue of re-marriage following the death of a spouse. He added a fascinating rider to his advice: 'I think that I too have the Spirit of God' (1 Corinthians 7:40). This phrase suggests that Paul had a moderate degree of conviction that he was communicating revelation given to him by the Holy Spirit, rather than simply giving well-reasoned advice. He was describing a subjective experience, the inner witness of the Spirit. It is even possible that he expected his readers to weigh his words and decide for themselves whether it was indeed a revelation concerning their current dilemma. We should also note that in this example the scope of prophecy extends to pastoral issues.

Like Paul, we can tentatively share our impressions with others and let them discern whether or not they seem to be from God. Paul's statement indicates that he was far from being certain and this gives us permission to be kind to ourselves and to others as we share what we believe *may* be from God. Wisdom from above is 'open to reason' rather than being a diktat (James 3:17). Sometimes 'open to reason' is translated as 'peaceable' which describes a non-combative stance in which we are easily persuaded.

## Seeing the Unseen

The term 'revelation' in the New Testament is *apokalypsis* from which we get the term apocalypse. It signifies that something that was obscure or hidden is now plainly seen, *unveiled*. We are familiar with how a sculpture is covered before being unveiled; once the covering is removed, the previously indistinct form is revealed to be a fully orbed creation. The revelatory activity of the Spirit can be described by the phrase 'seeing the unseen'. This is a function of our inner world, our spirit, so it differs from a merely intellectual appreciation of reality.

An example of seeing the unseen is found in the story of Elisha and his servant recounted in 2 Kings 6. They were surrounded by hostile forces and the servant was understandably extremely worried about their impending fate. Elisha, however, could see the unseen and prayed for his servant, 'O Lord, please open his eyes that he may see'. The veil was drawn aside and the servant saw the angelic armies of God arrayed on the hillside, ready for battle. He became aware of the unseen spiritual world which coexists with the 'natural world' in which we live.

Similarly, Jacob became aware of the previously veiled angelic presence at Bethel through a dream (Genesis 28:10-17). He saw what was actually there all along but was hidden from view until the point at which he received revelation. Seeing the unseen is not, strictly speaking, 'supernatural' knowledge. It is more a case of God making us aware of the reality of the spiritual realm which surrounds us.[13] Seeing the unseen – and communicating what we see to others – is the essence of prophecy. Because this is a subjective experience, it needs to be held lightly, tested, and weighed by others as none of us is infallible, however experienced we may be.

## Unspectacular Revelation

Sometimes revelation is accompanied by a particular feeling or sensation in a specific part of our body. People report a variety of experiences such as waves of heat passing through them, or a sense of heaviness in, for example, their calves. I occasionally have had this experience myself in the course of giving a talk, or during a conversation. I take this to indicate that I may need to say more about the point I am making. Much of the time, however, revelation is unspectacular and it creeps up on us unawares!

There may be occasions when we suddenly realise something about a situation or a person that is not based on observation or hearsay. It is not that we have thought deeply about the issue or person in question and have then worked towards a conclusion. The realisation simply

---

[13] I have written about this in greater depth in Cultivating God's Presence: Renewing Ancient Practices for Today's Church.

presents itself. This can be accompanied by a high degree of conviction and it can be an unsettling experience when you realise something and think to yourself 'but how do I know that?' The clarity which accompanies revelation makes it indistinguishable from the certainty accompanying other forms of knowledge. I usually find that this unspectacular form of revelation most often occurs when my eyes are open and I am actually looking at someone, rather than when I am praying.

In my early years as a Christian, I was filled with the Spirit. As I was praying in my bedroom, I had a sense of God's presence and unknown words formed in my mind. I assumed that this experience was mainly for my personal benefit, but I soon found that it had a wider impact. At this time, when looking at someone I would sometimes have a clear impression of what was on their mind. My intuitions were confirmed when, occasionally, I was able to tell them what they were thinking. At the time, I did not realise that this was unusual, as it felt natural rather than 'supernatural'. This was in my early 20s and I found it difficult to manage the emotional response which other people's thoughts sometimes evoked in me. Once I became aware that this was happening and being unable to manage the emotional side of it, I asked God to take this awareness away from me and he graciously did. I share this experience to emphasise how revelation can be received in quite unspectacular ways, indistinguishable from 'ordinary' knowledge acquired through conversation or observation.

I suspect that we often receive this sort of revelation but, because it is not accompanied by bells and whistles, we fail to realise that God is the source. Mature Christians often learn to be aware of their inner world and to take note of any thoughts that seem to come from left field. Perhaps an acquaintance repeatedly comes to mind for no obvious reason. This can at times be a prompt to pray for or contact the person concerned. At other times, a particular scripture might repeatedly intrude into our thoughts. God is often speaking, but we are not always listening!

How can we know which thoughts to take note of and which to ignore? I once received some very wise advice in conversation with a leader in the Catholic Charismatic Renewal. Her suggestion was to resist or ignore any repeated thoughts that we are uncertain about. If they originate from our psyche or represent a form of spiritual attack, they will likely fade over time ('resist the devil and he will flee from you'). But if they are from God they will probably intensify over time. This may sound counter-intuitive but it seems to work! Of course, if we have mental health issues or are under extreme stress, we may be dealing with unhealthy ruminations rather than revelation inspired by the Spirit. In such circumstances, we need to exercise caution and seek help from others, including discerning Christian friends and appropriate professional help.

## Fast Food vs Slow Cooking

Does the Spirit usually reveal things suddenly or is revelation more often received as a dawning awareness of something; in other words, is it a 'particular point in time' experience or a slower process which occurs over a period of time? This question is of practical importance, as some hyper-charismatic churches focus largely on 'on-the-spot' prophecy, but does this stack up to the witness of scripture?

Certainly, prophecy can involve an immediate experience, as described in 1 Corinthians 14:29-30. In this passage, Paul assumes that his readers are aware that the Spirit can move someone to prophesy when a revelation is suddenly given to that individual in a church gathering. He suggests that we make room for such contributions, the implication being that no one should hog the limelight during times of worship (1 Corinthians 14:30). Immediate revelation is the spiritual equivalent of fast food, prepared and delivered then and there, and best served fresh. But this is not the only way we can receive revelation – God can speak in many different ways.

Prophetic revelation can emerge slowly as the result of a long period spent seeking God. Peter writes that the prophets in the Old Testament *searched and enquired* and presumably this included searching the scriptures as well as time spent in prayer (1 Peter 1:10-12). The biblical prophets did not always deliver their prophecies immediately. It is also likely that they reflected on what they 'saw' or heard by way of revelation. Many of the prophecies we have recorded in the Bible are well-crafted pieces of literature and unless we believe that the prophets were essentially dictating machines, the polished final form of many prophecies suggests that they were finely honed in the interval between reception and delivery. In these instances, the final form of a prophecy can be seen as the result of an artistic, creative process in which God and humankind partner.

# 3

# Prophecy in Different Guises

For many, the term prophecy conjures up the image of someone communicating a concept or information in descriptive language (prose). Prose is excellent when we are primarily seeking to communicate such things. Several prophecies recorded in the Bible were delivered using straightforward prose, such as when Elijah predicted a prolonged famine in Israel (1 Kings 17:1). Prose is also widely used in the stories of Elisha, particularly when he provided strategic military advice.[14]

Prose may consist of a series of logical statements and can work at the level of rationality. This book consists largely of prose because it is a form of communication that is best suited for discussing ideas and concepts. Much contemporary prophecy is delivered using straightforward descriptive prose, but we should note that prose *was not* the dominant way in which biblical prophecy was communicated. There are circumstances where other ways and forms may be more effective.

Abraham Heschel provides us with a clue as to why prose is limited when it comes to many of the functions of prophecy. Heschel, a Jewish theologian, suggested that the majority of the Old Testament prophetic books were vehicles to communicate pathos, the sadness God feels about and towards his people and the world when things go awry.

Alongside pathos, the prophets communicated hope for the future. Sadness and hope need to be felt rather than understood intellectually.

---

[14] 'Prose' refers to any form of written or spoken language with a natural flow of speech. Works of philosophy, history, most fiction and journalism are written in prose.

They need to be *formed* within us, as opposed to our merely being *informed*.

Heschel's insights can help us reframe the purpose and value of much contemporary prophecy. Perhaps it is often less about communicating information and more about enabling us to feel what God feels and to see things from his perspective. If this is the case it is important that we utilise art and drama, poetry and song as these work more at the level of our emotions. Prose is certainly one way in which prophecy is communicated but are these other ways much in evidence today? The breadth of prophetic expression and action is considered in this chapter.

## Poetic language

> The overriding reality of the prophets is that they are characteristically poets.
> WALTER BRUEGGEMANN

Many biblical prophecies are poetic in nature. This does not mean that they are written in rhyming couplets although they may have a regular structure with verses based on metre and rhythm.[15] The term 'poetic' refers to the fact that much use is made of symbolic language and visual imagery to provoke a response that is deeper than intellect. Poetry principally employs the use of metaphorical language.

Metaphors can provide us with a helpful framework or lens through which to view situations or issues. The term 'metaphor' is derived from the Greek term for flasks, strapped to the side of a donkey to transport oil or wine. They simply functioned as vehicles and their pointed base meant they could not stand up unaided. A metaphor is similar in that it has no innate meaning aside from what it seeks to convey. For example, we might refer to someone having cold feet, being a couch potato or as happy as a clam. Although sometimes

---

[15] T S Eliot wrote that whereas 'the distinction between verse and prose is clear, the distinction between poetry and prose is obscure'. We have to be careful not to draw too clear a distinction. I am using the terms here to distinguish between more prosaic language that is primarily describing events or facts and that which employs metaphors, images and rhythm to make its point.

bizarre, metaphors are highly evocative, conjuring up images in our mind's eye. It has been said that an image is worth 10,000 words in terms of its powers of communication.

Metaphors work at the level of our imagination, transforming the way we see things. Biblical metaphors enable us to reframe our view of a situation by what, at first sight, might seem an illogical use of a familiar term. Isaiah employed the concept of fasting as a metaphor to highlight that caring for the poor is more important than religious observance (Isaiah 58). God is much more impressed with a fast from selfishness than with a fast from food.

Prophetic metaphors can be expressed in song or through actual poetry (rhyming or otherwise). Songwriters and poets often use creative imagery to forge hope in adversity. Rather than suggesting several good reasons from the Bible for getting involved with social justice, prophetic preaching captures our imagination and Amos's use of poetic language illustrates this well: 'Let justice roll down like waters and righteousness like a mighty stream'. If this were expressed in prose it might be something like: 'Justice must be widespread and righteousness must be powerful', in which case, so much meaning would be lost. Amos's poetry is much more vivid, and this verse was used with incredible power by Martin Luther King in his famous 'I have a dream' speech at the Lincoln Memorial. In fact, King is a prime example of someone who created and used poetry to great effect in his preaching.

Poetic imagery has the potential to *shape the hearts and minds* of all people. It can create hope in desperate situations when prose would struggle to do so. Compare these sentences:

- 'God cares for you and won't give up on you despite your poor behaviour.' PROSE

- 'How can I give you up, O Ephraim?... My heart recoils within me: my compassion grows warm and tender.' (Hosea 11:8). POETIC LANGUAGE

Which example communicates God's pathos most effectively? Which works at an intellectual level and which one pulls at our heartstrings and captures our imagination? It is this potential for prophecy to capture our imagination that makes it such an effective means of motivating the Church.

Sometimes church leaders, particularly those from highly missional or entrepreneurial churches, present plans for the future of their churches and then seek to recruit people to work towards the fulfilment of those plans. While this approach is sometimes appropriate and can have positive results, it is rare in such circumstances to find prophetic idioms being employed. The potential of prophetic imagery to create change by capturing people's imaginations is largely untapped.

When God's people were captives in Babylon, they needed to begin to trust God for their deliverance from their captors and for the restoration of Judah. They needed encouragement, renewal in their experience of God's presence, and stronger personal connections. Here is a plan, based on sound biblical and psychological principles, to achieve that goal:

- Get people to realise their condition, talking to them about how they have lost their homeland and pointing out that this has resulted in a bereavement reaction. Explain that their loss of hope is paralysing them.

- Start several connect groups so that people can come together and renew their connections in order to become an effective community.

- Create forums for prayer where people can experience healing, renewal and be infused with God's Spirit.

- Brainstorm ideas to forge a realistic plan for leaving Babylon and relocating to the Promised Land.

Does this sort of planning sound familiar? Here was how Ezekiel, having had a vision, approached this same challenge:

> The hand of the Lord was on me, and he brought me out in the Spirit of the Lord and set me down in the middle of the valley; it was full of bones... they were very dry. Then he said to me, 'Prophesy over these bones, and say to them, O dry bones, hear the word of the Lord'.
> Thus says the Lord God to these bones: 'Behold, I will cause breath to enter you, and you shall live. And I will lay sinews upon you and will cause flesh to come upon you, and cover you with skin

and put breath in you, and you shall live, and you shall know that I am the Lord.'

There was a sound, a rattling, and the bones came together, bone to its bone...

'I will open your graves and raise you from your graves, O my people, and I will bring you into the land of Israel... I will put my Spirit within you, and you shall live and I will place you in your own land.'

EZEKIEL 37:1-14 (SELECTED VERSES)

Which version, the logical plan or Ezekiel's vision, is more likely to encourage people by providing a vision of God's future? Which is more motivating and which allows for the creative unfolding of events (as opposed to pre-supposed outcomes)? Are the carefully crafted aims and objectives or the poetic imagery of Ezekiel's vision more likely to create hope?[16]

Prophecy can come in much plainer language and be received as a stimulus to planning, as we see in the case of Agabus's prediction of famine. This allowed a collection to be made to provide practical relief (Acts 11:27-30). It is not a case of *either* prophecy *or* planning. Just as there are prophetic gifts so there are gifts of administration given to the Church. Both are needed. Prophecy in the style of Agabus is most appropriate when facing issues where a definite course of action needs to be taken, whereas Ezekiel's style of prophecy is best suited to situations where hope and a renewal of faith are crucial.

## Prophetic Imagery

Visions, like poetic language, work at the level of our imagination and enable us to see and embrace truth on a spiritual and emotional level. In the late 1980s, having planted a small rural church, I felt quite pessimistic about its future and was continually turning over the question of its viability in my mind. A friend, unaware of my thoughts, shared a vision with me which sounded quite bizarre - actually like something out of a parody of the Charismatic Movement! The vision

---

[16] As a product of the Western Enlightenment, the logical plan may well feel more likely to succeed!

was of a fish tank with a fish skeleton floating in the middle of it. I knew immediately that it represented my tendency to ruminate (stare at the fish tank) and come up with a pessimistic conclusion (seeing only a skeleton). The humorous nature of the imagery helped me to lighten up and I heeded the warning which enabled me to continue to lead the church for 23 years. Without this prophetic image, I might well have packed it in at an early stage. I also suspect that a more directive approach ('I feel the Lord is encouraging you to continue') would not have helped me to change as my thought processes were so ingrained at that time. A prophetic image, arising from a dream or vision, can have an impact way beyond that of mere words.

Many prophecies in the Old Testament were, in fact, descriptions of visions. Joel's vision, which likened God's judgement to a plague of locusts, would have been a warning that hit home on a gut level, as his hearers would themselves have experienced the devastation that this would inevitably cause. A vision did more than simply inform Joel's hearers of impending judgement; it motivated them to change by evoking an emotional response to the reality of their plight.

When it comes to visions today, we need to exercise a degree of caution, as in some instances it may be more a question of 'visual thinking' rather than of revelation from God. A proportion of the population thinks in images rather than in words. A small percentage think almost wholly in this way and a larger number use visual thinking alongside thinking in words. When such people describe 'a picture', we may simply be witnessing their ability to see issues pictorially. That is not to denigrate the power of employing our imagination, as this is often an effective way, even the most effective way, to grasp reality, but we need to be careful not to regard all 'pictures' that people report as being prophetic images. When an image *is* from God what it symbolises will usually be evident to the person for whom it is intended even if it takes some time to become clear. The example that follows highlights that clarity can come almost immediately as well.

Several years ago, I was about to launch a two-year part-time leadership development programme called *Growing in Leadership*. Around this time, I attended a conference and received some prophetic input from an acquaintance who was unaware of my plans. He told me that he could visualise a tree and he felt that I needed to reach for the higher fruit. This tree/fruit metaphor caught my attention because the brochure for the course had a large tree on the front to represent the concept of growth. The prophecy encouraged me greatly, but why reach higher up? The fulfilment, reaching higher up, came some years later when I was appointed director of studies for a Master of Arts degree in Missional Leadership. This widened the scope of my engagement with leadership development, enabling me to produce and deliver course content to church leaders from many different streams and denominations. Prophetic images can powerfully align us with, or confirm, God's will for our lives.

## Prophetic Enactment

The biblical prophets employed prose and poetic language to communicate their revelation, but they sometimes delivered their message by dramatically enacting or actually living out the word of the Lord.

Prophetic enactment was often costly, involving great personal risk, and was sometimes quite bizarre. Isaiah, for example, walked naked around Jerusalem for three years (how would we cope with that today?!) Jeremiah hid a waistband in a cleft in a rock. Ezekiel had to deny himself any form of public mourning for the death of his wife (Isaiah 20, Jeremiah 13, Ezekiel 24). Hosea married an unfaithful wife to be a visual demonstration of God's relationship with his people in the face of Israel's unfaithfulness. These are extreme examples of people who had a clear call to prophetic ministry but there are lessons to be learned from their example. In these instances, prophecy involved the whole being of the prophet.

The biblical prophets were, like Jesus, incarnational in living out what they brought, at huge personal cost. Prophecy cannot be detached from our daily lives in the public arena. The prophet as a detached observer or seer is a model promoted in some charismatic circles, but this is far from what we see in the Bible. Many embraced the risk inherent in their powerlessness, putting their necks on the line, and provoking a confrontation with the powers that be. This is important to take into account when considering topics such as prophecy and politics or prophecy as it relates to spiritual warfare. Prophecy in the Bible was certainly not an armchair exercise as it risked opposition and overt persecution. This, according to Jesus, was how 'the prophets who were before you' were received and a truly prophetic church – one that lives out, and enacts, its prophetic message - should expect a similar reception (Matthew 5:12).

In summary, the biblical prophets sought to communicate the heart and will of God in a variety of ways. At times this was in the form of prose, sometimes giving specific direction but more commonly, figurative language was used. The biblical prophets used 'poetic' metaphors, designed to communicate feeling not just facts and frequently used imagery, including dreams and visions. Dramatic enactment and actually living out the message was another way in which the prophets brought the word of God to bear on their hearers. They used everything within their power, under God's hand, to get their message across.

## Subversive Prophecy

Why do we need prophecy today? One reason is that we tend to be blind to the reality that surrounds us and are in need of a wake-up call. We are often unaware that the status quo (which is Latin for *the mess we are in*) is not the way things should be. We become so familiar with our surroundings that it takes a revelation to wake us up and be able to see things more clearly. This is reminiscent of the old joke where one fish asks another, 'How's the water today?' The other fish replies, 'What's water?'

Prophetic images and poetic language can create change by first disrupting the way in which we currently perceive the present. Sometimes this prophetic disruption, never comfortable, is the only route that will lead to change. Nathan the prophet stood before David and told him a story about a stolen lamb. David was moved to anger by this narrative before he realised that it described the nature of his own sin. This was an extremely disturbing event for David, challenging his attitude of entitlement. Once David realised that *he* was the thief in the story it created the possibility for deep and lasting change (2 Samuel 12:1-4).

Jesus also used stories to subvert the views of his hearers; the Good Samaritan was an oxymoron (by definition no Samaritan could ever be good). This story undermined all that the Pharisees held dear - more effectively than would have been the case if Jesus had employed a rational argument. Stories work at the level of our imagination, creating mental images, which, once seen, are unforgettable – we cannot unsee them.

I enjoy listening to and playing music, particularly the blues. Music conforms to particular scales, such as the familiar and happy major scales. Less familiar are what are known as modes, which represent variations on scales. Modes are named after regions in Greece and my favourite is the Aeolian Mode (a minor scale). It is said of the Aeolian Mode that it can reach the depths of our being without disturbing the surface. It reaches us on a deep, often unconscious, level. Prophecy is God's version of the Aeolian Mode, employing metaphors and images relevant to our culture which manage to cut through our rational defences and reach the very depths of our beings.

The idea that prophecy continues to be an important aspect of church life today is contested by those who are convinced that the Bible teaches us that prophecy has ceased. This debate is important to address and forms the topic of the next chapter.

# 4

# Is Prophecy Operative Today?

> Love never ends. *As for prophecies, they will pass away*; as for tongues, they will cease; as for knowledge, it will pass away.
> 1 CORINTHIANS 13:8

Some Christians have misgivings about prophecy being for today. It is important not only to acknowledge such reservations but to consider them thoughtfully.

- There are those who suggest that accounts of prophecy in the Bible are akin to religious myth with little or no historical basis. In this view, the suggestion that prophetic gifts are operative today is a form of delusion or superstitious thinking. Those who hold such views struggle to acknowledge or believe that God's power operates either through prophecy, or healing or miraculous happenings of any kind. While it is true that deception or psychological factors may be involved in some accounts of prophecy, there are many stories of contemporary prophecy in circulation that, over the course of time, have proven to be genuine in people's experience. With many varied examples available for scrutiny there is a considerable weight of evidence in favour of the genuineness of at least some contemporary prophecy.

- Others argue that although prophecy was crucial in biblical times, it is no longer needed now that we have the New Testament to guide us; that it has, in fact, already 'passed away' just as Paul said it would (1 Corinthians 13:8). In this view, the charismatic dimension of life in the Spirit, involving prophecy, healing and speaking in tongues, is no longer applicable. The role of the Holy Spirit then concerns the conviction of sin, conversion and assurance of salvation, as well as bringing revelation and guidance through scripture. This is the view of those known as 'Cessationists'.

'Cessationist' is a term derived from the word 'cease'. I have some sympathy with this view, particularly in the light of a small minority of Charismatics who regard contemporary prophecy as being on par with the Bible. Although in theory this may be denied, in practice such people give more attention to what the Lord may be saying today than to the revelation contained in scripture. This includes some 'prophets' seen on YouTube who suggest that to disbelieve their prophetic words is tantamount to disobeying God, thereby placing their revelation on the same level as that of scripture. This is erroneous.

The Bible is uniquely authoritative, its authority being far above that of any man or woman living today, however gifted they may be. We should not regard any person as being infallible and Paul warned us that we need to be on our guard against being dazzled by the brilliance of the messenger (Galatians 1:8). These negative examples represent only a small charismatic fringe and, although deeply concerning, they should not lead us to despise prophecy.

Many Cessationists do, however, allow for the continuation of apparently less spectacular gifts, such as teaching and acts of mercy (Romans 12:6-8); not that the fruit of such gifts could, in any way, be considered unspectacular. The reasoning behind why certain gifts continued and others have ceased is somewhat difficult to follow.

## The Witness of Church History

Cessationists base their belief that prophecy, healing, tongues and words of knowledge have died out on presumed absence of evidence that they persisted in the history of the Church. But does this view bear scrutiny?

The view that the miraculous had ceased was not held until the time of the Reformation and is, therefore, a relatively recent teaching. Its origin can be traced to the sixteenth century when Martin Luther was challenged by certain Catholic theologians who demanded that he prove his authority by working miracles. He held to his view that scripture alone, not miracles, is the source of authority for doctrine. Luther was not actually discounting the miraculous – he was simply refusing to support his arguments from anything other than the Bible. However, his statement, designed to affirm scripture, was taken to extremes by some prominent Reformers, resulting in a rejection of the gifts of the Spirit. Yet this is far from Luther's own position - he believed in divine healing and some of his followers reported that he prophesied.

In the early twentieth century, the influential theologian B B Warfield stated categorically that all contemporaneous miracles were counterfeit. He was convinced that none had occurred since the time of the 12 apostles, despite well-documented evidence that prophetic gifts were still in operation well into the post-apostolic period.[17]

The *Didache* can be cited as confirmation of the persistence of such gifts. This document, written at the end of the first or beginning of the second century, discussed the ministry of prophets and apostles in some detail and outlined principles by which churches could discern who was a genuine prophet and who was a charlatan. The content of the *Didache* confirms that there was an ongoing prophetic ministry after the time of the Twelve and that the author accepted that at least some prophecy was genuine. Similarly, Irenaeus described a variety of gifts that were still in operation in the second century:

> In like manner, we do also hear many brethren in the Church, who possess prophetic gifts, and who through the Spirit speak all kinds of languages and bring to light for the general benefit the hidden things of men and declare the mysteries of God.
> AGAINST HERESIES

This description of charismatic ministry sounds as if it was taken straight from the book of Acts. There is no hint that spiritual gifts were fading or had died out.

Justin Martyr, a Christian in Rome in the mid-second century, wrote along the same lines:

---

[17] Josh Hoffert of Wind Ministries has produced a very informative study guide documenting the persistence of prophecy in the early centuries of the Church. https://www.windministries.ca/blog/category/The%20Prophecy%20Series

> The prophetical gifts remain with us, even to the present time. And hence you ought to understand that [the gifts] formerly among your nation [Israel] have been transferred to us.

Further examples of prophetic gifts are numerous and some are recounted in subsequent chapters. Cessationists also cite their own experience in defence of their views, asking: if prophecy continues into the present day, why is it absent from so many Bible-affirming churches?[18] One possible implication is that prophecy only exists in charismatic circles as a form of auto-suggestion and that those involved convince themselves that their thoughts and intuitions are actually forms of revelation. This line of reasoning overlooks the fact that the Bible emphasises that our desire for these gifts is an important element in their reception: we are encouraged to *ask* God to give us gifts of revelation, including that of the gift of wisdom (James 1:5-6). The scriptural injunction to *earnestly desire* prophecy suggests that we may fail to receive such revelation if we do not seek it wholeheartedly (1 Corinthians 14:1). Similarly, Jesus encouraged people to actively seek the presence of the Holy Spirit, rather than to take a more passive approach (Luke 11:9-13). One reason for the evident lack of prophecy in Cessationist churches may be that, once people have dismissed the possibility of spiritual gifts, expectations are low and faith to receive them is non-existent. Lack of faith or resistance due to our theological understanding can easily quench the Spirit. Sometimes we do not have simply because we do not ask.

In other instances, prophetic and other gifts are received, but under a different name. Cessationists may, for example, pray for healing, but would be reluctant to label this as seeking a *gift* of healing. I came to faith in my teens through a Baptist church. Despite the lack of teaching on spiritual gifts, I was aware that the minister had heard an audible voice directing him to ordination. This occurred when he was onboard a ship in the Royal Navy, in the days before the Charismatic Movement.

---

[18] Although experience is a source of religious knowledge, it is difficult to mount a convincing argument from the absence of certain experiences. There may be many reasons why we fail to receive prophetic gifts, other than their availability, as is evident in 1 Samuel 3:1.

However, most Cessationists do believe that God guides us, and so do allow for some forms of contemporary revelation - it has been suggested by some that this is simply prophecy under another name. We might also consider the example of Duncan Campbell, the prime mover in the Hebridean Revival which took place in 1949. Campbell went to the Isle of Lewis because two ladies in their 80s had prayed and sensing an intense presence of the Lord, became convinced that God was going to send revival. The two sisters were so convinced, in fact, that they sent a telegram to the Faith Mission on the Isle of Lewis requesting that Campbell be sent to their island.[19] The events that followed suggest that they were indeed prompted by the Holy Spirit as there were many remarkable stories of spontaneous mass conversions. Revelation was a crucial ingredient in these examples, even if those at the time would not have used charismatic terminology to describe it.

## Has Prophecy Ceased?

> Love never ends. As for prophecies, they will pass away... for we know in part and we prophesy in part, but when the perfect comes, the partial will pass away.
> 1 CORINTHIANS 13:8-11

As well as looking to church history, Cessationists seek support for their views in certain biblical passages, especially in Paul's statement that prophecy will one day 'pass away'. They argue that the phrase 'when the perfect comes' refers to the time when the New Testament was completed. In their view, the sole purpose of prophecy was to guide the Church up to the point when the written word of God existed. Now that the Church has the scriptures, they argue, prophecy is no longer necessary. One problem with this argument concerns determining the date we accept for the completion of the New Testament - not an easy task. The Gospels and letters were written in the first century and were initially circulated as individual books, or fragments, rather than as the complete New Testament. In addition, an agreement on which books should be accepted as scripture (the Canon)

---

[19] https://ifphc.wordpress.com/2021/11/18/duncan-campbell-and-the-hebrides-revival-1949-1952/

was reached much later, in the fourth century (although there is still no complete agreement between Catholics, Orthodox and Protestants about which books constitute Christian scripture).

The suggestion that the Bible is described as 'the perfect' is somewhat strained, even if the psalmist regarded the Law as being perfect in his day. In his famous description of scripture, Paul used the much less superlative term 'useful' to describe it (2 Timothy 3:16). The most natural reading of 'when the perfect comes' is that it is a phrase that refers to the second coming of Jesus.

I spend much time reading and studying the Bible and cannot value it highly enough, yet I would like to believe that when Jesus, the living Word, returns, our knowledge of God will be on a whole new (face-to-face) level. At that point, we will require neither prophecy nor scripture to help us know what God is like. Instead, we will be able to say with Job, 'I had heard of you by the hearing of the ear, but now my eye sees you' (Job 42:5).

A variation on this argument is the suggestion that the apostles were endowed with gifts such as healing and prophecy to authenticate them as witnesses and authors of scripture. This argument is flawed on several counts, including the fact that Philip, a deacon who left no writings of his own, saw many miracles in Samaria (Acts 8:4-8). In this case, healing and deliverance were unrelated to the need to prove the authenticity of the writers of the New Testament.

Prophecy is a form of communication from God that is temporary but necessary in this age. Prophetic gifts fulfil a similar role to emails, letters and postcards; they are effective ways of communicating when we cannot see someone in person. However, it is worth saying that I am unlikely to email my friend when we are sitting in the same room together! In the same way, when we see God face-to-face, there will be no further need of prophecy and 'prophecies will pass away'.

## Peter Declared that Prophecy Would Continue

Ultimately it is scripture itself that convinces us that prophecy has a vital role to play until the end of this age. Peter interpreted the Day of Pentecost using Joel's prophecy to explain the significance of the events he witnessed and, if we take his words seriously, we will regard prophecy as a normal and ongoing feature of church life:

> And in the last days it shall be, God declares, that I will pour out my Spirit on all flesh, and your young men shall see visions, and your old men shall dream dreams; even on my male servants and female servants *in those days I will pour out my Spirit, and they shall prophesy.*

He went on to explain that the promise of forgiveness *and* the promise of the Holy Spirit, giving rise to prophecy, will continue indefinitely:

> ...for the promise is for you and your children *and for all who are far off*, everyone whom the Lord our God calls to himself.
> ACTS 2:17-18, 39

The phrase 'all who are far off' signifies distant generations to come embracing everyone who has been called by God, the entire company of God's people. Peter considered that prophecy, dreams and visions would continue unabated down through successive generations of the Church. The Spirit of prophecy is promised to every spiritual descendant of those first believers. The outpouring of God's Spirit in this current age gives rise to gifts of revelation, gifts that are vital for the Church to continue the ministry of Jesus.

Jesus promised that those who believe in him will experience rivers of life flowing 'out of their innermost being' (John 7:37-39). This was a picture of the activity of the life-giving Spirit of God who speaks to us and through us. The link between the presence of the Spirit and the gift of prophecy is evident in several passages in Acts. Arriving in Ephesus, Paul laid hands on certain followers of John the Baptist who possessed only a rudimentary knowledge of Jesus. The outcome was that they received an outpouring of the Spirit of prophecy. Having accepted the testimony of Paul (which would later be enshrined in scripture) they experienced the reality of God for themselves (Acts 19:6).

The Bible contains many examples of what we ourselves might expect to see in contemporary prophecy. These are the so-called non-canonical prophets who did not write scripture. Their prophecies had no universal application beyond their time, unlike those of Isaiah, Hosea or John the author of Revelation. Agabus, on the other hand, received revelation that related only to his immediate context and, therefore, there is no *Book of Agabus* in the New Testament. Contemporary prophets are more like Agabus than those prophets who had the God-given authority to write scripture.

## The Distinct & Unique Role of the Bible

Along with my Cessationist brothers and sisters, I strongly affirm that the Bible plays a unique role in the life of the Church. The Bible, not contemporary prophecy, is the source of orthodoxy (right beliefs) and orthopraxy (right living). Although prophecy today may *illuminate* our understanding of doctrine, it can never *add to* our understanding of doctrine, nor can it provide us with the framework for the practical outworking of our faith. Biblical revelation is authoritative in a way that contemporary prophecy is not. If I had to choose between having prophecy or the Bible there would be no contest - the Bible would win, hands down.

The Bible consists of a library of 66 books (in the Protestant canon) which encompass several different literary genres. It describes the history of God's people and contains eyewitness accounts of the life of Jesus, his teaching, death and resurrection. The Bible is the primary source for our knowledge about God, the life of faith, morality and doctrine. It is invaluable and many martyrs have willingly given their lives so that we might have the scriptures freely available to us today. The Bible invites us into fellowship with the triune God: Father, Son and Holy Spirit. When it is interpreted with skill and knowledge it establishes the parameters for our life in God. As Paul wrote:

> All scripture is inspired by God and profitable for teaching, for reproof, for correction, for training in righteousness; so that the man of God may be complete, equipped for every good work.
> 2 TIMOTHY 3:16-17

Books were included in the Bible because they seemed to be *qualitatively* different from other writings, however helpful those writings were. Genesis, Isaiah, Matthew's Gospel, etc., have been regarded as scripture down the millennia. The formation of the Canon of scripture was a process of community discernment - representatives of the whole Church decided which books were uniquely authoritative. Several other books that were written around the same time as the New

Testament, such as *The Shepherd of Hermas* and *The Didache*, were also highly regarded. They were seen as helpful guides to Christian living but not considered to be scripture. Similarly, today we have many helpful Christian books, but no one confuses the authority of Amos with that of C S Lewis. Yet both the Bible and C S Lewis have a role to play, albeit an unequal one. It is a similar situation concerning the relationship between scripture and contemporary prophecy – both are important, but they have different roles. Scripture and prophecy are complementary rather than in competition with each other. We need both the Word *and* the Spirit.

5

# The Unique Role of Prophecy

## An Example of Prophecy Today

Contemporary prophecy and the Bible have different functions. Prophecy helps us to become more clearly aware of God's will for our lives. It can also heighten our awareness of his involvement in our past, our present and in our future. The following story illustrates this:

In 1998, I was driving with my wife to a Christian leadership conference. Our conversation centred on our need for a break to recharge our batteries. At the time, I was working part-time for the National Health Service, alongside leading a rural church established some years previously. We had come through a challenging time and were finding that balancing the demands of the church, work and family was weighing heavily upon us.

In addition, we were seeking to understand ourselves and one another better having worked through several issues over the previous years. Although the outcome had been positive, the process had taken its toll. As we drove up the motorway, we finally came to the sad conclusion that a break was not feasible, not only because of lack of finances but also because of the practical issue of who would look after our children while we were away. The speaker at the conference was unknown to us. We found it easy to listen to his American drawl - he came from North Carolina near the Old Smokey Mountain (of 'On Top of Old Smokey' fame).

After one talk, he asked me to come to the front of the gathering and suggested that my wife should join me. He then proceeded to tell us that we each needed to appreciate more fully the way in which the Holy Spirit moves in the other. This was spot on - opposites attract and we have very different personalities. It seemed very pertinent to our recent experience although no doubt true of many couples and it could have been nothing more than a good guess! However, he then went on to say something which greatly surprised us. He told us that on our journey to the conference we had been discussing the possibility of having a break together, which, of course, we had been. He went on to say that this was not optional, it was an actual necessity. He concluded by telling us that God would provide the necessary finance and also that he would look after our children. We were astounded, as only my wife and I knew about the conversation in the car, and also we couldn't think how it could possibly work out in reality.

The very evening we returned home, we received a call from my wife's brother, who knew nothing of our time at the conference. He told us that he wanted to take our three children to EuroDisney near Paris. This amazed us as no one had ever made such an offer before. He said that he would finance the trip and that we could choose any time we liked. A few days later we received two financial gifts. One was from somebody who had been at the conference and another was from a couple who had heard about the prophecy. Encouraged, we booked a break in a small hotel in the Cotswolds and arranged for the children's EuroDisney trip to take place over the same period. When we came to pay the hotel bill for our break it came to the exact amount that we had been given by our friends (in fact, it cost 50 pence more than the amount we had been given, so I have always felt that God owes us 50 pence!) This series of events was meaningful far beyond our having a much-needed time away. It helped me realise that God really did care deeply about us and brought home to me the fact that 'his steadfast love endures forever'.

This prophetic word involved several different dimensions of the prophetic gift. It included knowledge of a conversation held in private ('a word of knowledge'); insight concerning interpersonal dynamics (again 'a word of knowledge'); and the prediction of future events which were fulfilled to the last detail ('a prophecy' as traditionally understood).

## Prophecy in the New Testament

The role of prophecy in the life of the Church is illustrated by examining how it functioned in New Testament times. The following examples demonstrate that the role of prophecy differs from the role of scripture:

### Prophecy can warn of coming events

> Now in these days, prophets came down from Jerusalem to Antioch. And one of them named Agabus stood up and foretold by the Spirit that there would be a great famine over all the world (this took place in the days of Claudius).
> ACTS 11:27-28

Agabus predicted a famine, enabling the Church to create a fund to provide relief for those who would soon be in need. Imagine if Agabus had not predicted the famine but that the believers had a copy of the (as yet unwritten) New Testament. Would having scripture have made this warning unnecessary? In the same way, Joseph, using dream interpretation, was able to inform Pharoah of an impending famine. This meant that food could be collected and stored in the seven years of abundance which would precede the seven years of failed harvests. Would possessing the Bible have rendered the need for these warnings unnecessary? Of course not!

Agabus's prophetic ministry performed a different function from that of scripture. It was related to a time-limited set of circumstances. His prophetic word did not establish a pattern for right living or right beliefs; neither did it provide a universal template for how we should approach famines. It is, however, of more than purely historical interest; it is an example of what we ourselves might expect to happen at different times because we follow the same God whom we see revealed in scripture.

### Prophecy can set us on the right course (or confirm it)

Scripture sets us on the right course when moral issues are involved. Often, however, life's decisions revolve around two or more legitimate options and in these circumstances, we need discernment as to which course to take. Alongside taking advice and weighing up our options, Christians usually seek guidance from God through prayer, sometimes through a discernment process and sometimes through prophetic input. This is because prophecy may actually indicate the broad outline of God's will for our lives and ministries, as we see in operation in Paul's exhortation in 1 Timothy 1:18:

> This charge I entrust to you, Timothy, my child, *in accordance with the prophecies previously made about you*, that by them you may wage the good warfare...

The prophecies given to Timothy were narrow in their focus, relating only to one specific individual. In contrast, the Bible is not, like prophecy, time-limited and situation-specific (2 Timothy 3:16).

The obvious lesson to be drawn from the example of Timothy is that we should be open to prophetic guidance. Scripture will not provide us with such specificity when we consider our particular vocation. The fact that we have the Bible does not exclude our own need for the type of revelation given to encourage and direct Timothy.

## Prophecy can help us see the consequences of our plans

Agabus appears again in Acts 21. Paul was planning a trip to Jerusalem. Agabus removed Paul's belt and used it to tie his own hands and feet telling him, 'This is how the Jews at Jerusalem will bind the man who owns this belt...' As far as Agabus was concerned this indicated that Paul should not go to Jerusalem because he was in danger of being taken captive. Paul, the recipient of the prophecy, accepted it as being accurate but, unlike Agabus, took it as an encouragement to go to Jerusalem. To Agabus it was a warning – to Paul, it was a confirmation because he was ready to die for the sake of Jesus.

This story illustrates a very important point: *prophecy is never telling another person what to do*. Genuine prophecy never usurps an individual's freedom to choose. The recipient of a prophecy has the final say and, therefore, the person concerned takes full responsibility for how to respond to it. How to act on a prophetic word is wholly between the individual and God.

Again, we see that Agabus' ministry has a different role to play than that of scripture. This difference is often overlooked by those who believe that spiritual gifts died out in the early Christian centuries. We need prophetic insights to guide us in our decisions - no less than did those early believers.

## Prophecy can bring encouragement & affirmation

Prophecies can warn us or outline God's will for our future but more often they are designed to be words of encouragement. A prophetic word can simply communicate to the recipient that God is aware of them and their situation. When Jesus met Nathanael he was able to tell him two things: the first was that his integrity had been noticed; he then told Nathanael exactly what he had been doing just before their meeting (John 1:45-51). This was not a prophecy in the sense of prediction but what is commonly referred to as 'a word of knowledge'.

I have wondered what it must have been like for Nathanael to receive these words from Jesus which undoubtedly were a revelation from God. I suspect that they made him aware that God not only noticed him, but that also he was appreciated, cared for and loved. The New Testament is the primary means by which we know that God is aware of us and loves us, but at times a more direct and personal form of communication greatly helps. This is particularly the case when we are very low in spirits or if we have a very negative image of ourselves. We should never despise those very simple prophecies that simply state that God loves us.

Prophecy is also given to groups, as well as to individuals, in order to build them up (edify), comfort and encourage them (1 Corinthians 14:3). We can see an example of this in Acts 15:23:

> And Judas and Silas, who were themselves prophets, *encouraged and strengthened* the brothers with many words.

Unfortunately, there is no detailed description of their ministry. I would like to know, for example, whether they encouraged the believers with specific prophecies. They may simply have delivered more general teaching tailored (prophetically) to the circumstances of their audience. There is just as much need for this form of prophetic ministry today, a ministry that renews hope and creates courage.

## Prophecy can capture our imagination

Dreams and visions sometimes employ imaginative imagery to communicate their message. This is similar to those sections of the New Testament that are described as 'apocalyptic literature' (apocalyptic means 'revelation'). Apocalyptic literature uses the same technique as modern political cartoons found in newspapers. If, for instance, you saw a cartoon with a large bear grasping a dove it would suggest that Russia (the bear) was seeking to destroy peace (indicated by the dove). The bear has a timeless meaning (danger) but today it has a more focused meaning, as it commonly represents Russia. We understand what the cartoon is seeking to convey because we know what the symbols represent.

The book of Revelation, some sections of Peter's letters and Matthew 24 all fall into the category of apocalyptic writing. In the ancient Near East, this was a common form of writing, using heavily-coded vivid imagery to communicate hope in adversity. It is similar to what is seen in Daniel and several other Old Testament prophets.

At the time these prophecies were written most people would have had little difficulty understanding their symbolism and would easily grasp the coded message they conveyed. When we read these prophecies today, we need to dig deep to understand the meaning the symbols would convey at the time they were written. Otherwise, we end up with some very odd ideas.[20] Dreams and visions today often employ contemporary imagery and because we can relate to this it can have great impact. How we interpret the imagery we see in modern-day dreams and visions is explored in more detail later.

Having looked at the unique role of prophecy, we will now turn to practical issues, such as who can prophesy and the best way to deliver a prophecy.

---

[20] Any serious student of John's Revelation would benefit from reading Richard Bauckham's *The Book of Revelation*. It contains a wealth of information about apocalyptic symbolism based on extensive research.

6

# The Who & How of Prophecy

Back in the 1970s over a period of 2-3 years, I had a fruitful sojourn in a very welcoming Pentecostal church. I had the desire to learn more about how the Spirit moves in a congregation and although many of my friends were becoming involved in the emerging Charismatic Movement and forming new churches, I reckoned that Pentecostals had many years of experience of the Spirit. I wanted to draw on their experience and this particular church became my school of the Spirit.

There were times when the Spirit of prophecy seemed to rest heavily on this working-class congregation. Someone would spontaneously start a song or a hymn and another person would read a scripture which often fitted well with the song; there might be prophecy or tongues with interpretation, all following a similar theme. Orchestrated by the Spirit, the congregation was led in the same direction, as if a divine conductor were bringing different instruments into play, one after the other. Two sweet elderly ladies would often cut across this process by singing their favourite chorus, 'God is still on the throne, and he will remember his own…'! Despite this endearing distraction, I learned to be aware of the dynamics of the Spirit moving in and through a congregation.

## Who Can Prophesy?

Paul encouraged his readers to seek spiritual gifts which suggest that they are available to every Christian: '…earnestly desire the spiritual gifts, especially that you may prophesy' (1 Corinthians 14:1).

Paul's words suggest that prophecy is available to the many not just the few. John Wimber summarised this potential in his famous phrase, 'Everyone can play'. In his view, we all should expect to receive spiritual gifts, including prophecy, even if this is just an occasional experience.

Paul gave priority to prophecy above all other gifts. The fact that he was emphatic in his exhortation to desire prophecy indicates that it is an important gift that is open to everyone in the Church. Paul had no difficulty with women praying and prophesying in public alongside men, as long as they used their freedom wisely. This was not an expression of gender bias as the same principle applied to men, who were also expected to conform to what was culturally acceptable (see 1 Corinthians 11:4-5).

Paul emphasised that love is the most important thing for Christians, with prophecy being mentioned in the same breath. It is not a question of either/or but of both/and; we are to pursue both love and prophecy. This is because our words can have such a positive impact; they can build others up, encourage and strengthen people in their faith (1 Corinthians 14:3). The structure of 1 Corinthians 12-14 is instructive: chapter 12 looks at the place of spiritual gifts in Christ's body; chapter 13 counters our tendency to pride to ensure that we exercise our gifts in the context of love; chapter 14 emphasises the role of prophecy (and speaking in tongues). The implication of this sequence is that prophecy is a primary way in which we can serve others. Along with other spiritual gifts, prophecy is an expression of love in action.

By encouraging us to seek prophecy above all other gifts, it is unlikely that Paul was suggesting that we should all become the sort of prophets who stand up before a congregation and declare with great authority 'thus saith the Lord…' It is more likely that his exhortation was to share our God-given intuitions and insights, to pray for others according to the leading of the Spirit and to share 'pictures', both distinct visions and more vague impressions concerning individuals or groups of people. Prophecy can also take the form of encouragement, as the Spirit supplies the words we need to strengthen others in their resolve to follow the Lord (Acts 15:32).

Alongside the potential of every believer to prophesy, some will exercise a more specialised ministry. Such people regularly prophesy and may exercise other related gifts, such as words of knowledge. Having greater experience in the operation of these gifts is likely to result in a higher-than-average degree of skill and accuracy. This more specialised prophetic ministry usually follows a clear call to bring God's word to individuals and churches. We cannot appoint someone to this ministry as it depends wholly on God's choosing (Jeremiah 1:5).[21]

## The Relational Context for Prophecy

It is important to note that prophecy in the New Testament was usually, if not entirely, delivered in the context of existing relationships. The early church strongly emphasised the importance of relational bonds and although there are other metaphors for the Church such as body, temple and bride, the dominant framework by far is that of family-type relationships. This is evidenced by the frequent use of terms such as brother, sister, father and mother in Paul's letters. In view of this, we might ask whether predictive or directive prophecy should ever be exercised outside of a clear relational context, as this contrasts with what is seen in the New Testament.[22]

The same emphasis on relationship is evident in the book of Revelation where the author addressed his prophecy to those whom he knew intimately. The seven churches to which he wrote were subject to his ongoing care and he would have had close kinship relationships with his readers. John's prophetic word was specific to individual congregations each of which was well-known to him. Each had its unique context and faced its own challenges ranging from persecution to lukewarmness or heretical teaching. John's prophetic ministry, like that of Paul, was relational, exercised through kinship rather than through a hierarchical structure: 'I, John, your *brother* and *partner*...' (Revelation 1:9).

---

[21] Even in the case of Isaiah, a willingness to be God's spokesperson was not enough and he could not 'go' and speak God's word until God had commissioned him (Isaiah 6:8-9).

[22] Some readers may object to this thought given some examples of Old Testament prophecy. The context for prophecy in Israel was, however, somewhat different to that of the Church, as will be examined later.

We would expect to see a relational context for prophecy today and most prophetic ministry will be exercised in a local church, or group of churches. Those prophesying will, therefore, normally be known by and accountable to others in their locality. We are wise to ensure that any 'extra-local ministers' (prophetic or otherwise) are well-known and respected for their personal qualities in their own context.

## Celebrity Prophets

A pattern has emerged in the age of the internet whereby 'prophets' with mass audiences disseminate their prophecies far and wide. Many of these may be considered to have become Christian celebrities. Being a celebrity is somewhat different from simply being famous. As Katelyn Beaty has pointed out in her book on Christian celebrity culture, celebrities are influential and they exert their social power without 'proximity'. In other words, they have charisma and gain a devoted following, but they are not personally known to their followers.

Christian celebrity culture is diametrically opposed to the situation we see in the New Testament, where Paul insists that authority should result from sacrificial living rather than from any personal charisma. It was his suffering that confirmed his calling, along with the fruit seen in the lives of those in the churches he founded. His emphasis was on the hardships he had endured, rather than how impressive he was in person (2 Corinthians 10:1-12:10; 13:5-7).

The issue of discernment and weighing prophecy is difficult in a celebrity culture. All forms of revelation should be offered tentatively; none is to be automatically accepted as authentic and each contribution needs to be 'weighed' (1 Corinthians 14:29). Who discerns the accuracy of prophecies disseminated by individuals who are only known through their videos and who, therefore, are relative strangers to their audience? This is especially important where prophecies are predictive or directive in nature. Who calls those concerned to account if their prediction proves to be false? Devoted followers are usually not the best people to provide such accountability.

There are others considered to be prophets who exercise internet ministries consisting mainly of biblical teaching. They may be drawing on scripture to share what they feel is relevant to a current issue or they may want to encourage viewers to put down deeper roots in God's love. This is a legitimate and wholly worthwhile pursuit but is closer to teaching, rather than being prophetic ministry.

## Itinerant Prophets

A similar issue relates to how we approach itinerant ministers who might prophesy to congregations geographically spread. It is wise to exercise caution when prophets are unknown to us personally or to others in our context. If someone with a wide geographical ministry comes to a conference or a church, we would expect certain safeguards to be in place. He or she should at least be known by those in leadership, and they should be accountable within their own denomination or church network. The essential factor is whether such people have close enough relationships with others to be known.

Jesus indicated that, rather than a spectacular ministry, *the fruit of our lives* is proof of authenticity, including the fruit of any prophecy given (Matthew 7:20). To be aware of the fruit resulting from someone's life we need to experience everyday life together (rather than simply believing that person's publicity). Jesus went on to describe the situation where some prophesied in his name, even though he regarded them as being 'lawless' (Matthew 7:21-23). To be lawless implies that they are independent, self-styled and accountable to neither God nor man.

This is not a new issue, as roving prophets were a challenge in the period immediately following the time of the Apostles. This difficult situation was addressed in the *Didache*, an early Christian document written somewhere between AD 80 and 120. Itinerant Christian preachers were travelling from church to church and claiming to be either prophets or apostles.

The *Didache* provided criteria for judging such people's ministry. If, for example, they seemed mainly interested in financial gain, or if their prophecy was centred on themselves, they were likely to be false apostles or prophets. Today we are also aware of other negative motives such as personal ambition or the desire to attract a following. We might also be more attuned to the presence of narcissistic personality traits in those who prophesy.

## The Language of Prophecy

We now turn to the topic of *how* we deliver prophecy in practice. When I was in the Pentecostal church it was customary for prophetic words to begin with 'thus saith the Lord' or 'I the Lord'. This reflected the fact that many of the congregation had been raised with the language of the Authorised Version of the Bible. These phrases signalled that the speaker was prophesying, rather than just sharing a bright idea. But the following factors need to be considered:

- When these sorts of phrases were used by the Old Testament prophets, they were utilising a form of speech that their contemporaries would easily recognise as the preamble to a prophecy. Formulaic phrases, such as 'thus saith the Lord' or 'the word of the Lord came to me', were common and they would have been recognised in pagan circles as well as in Israelite religion. They were familiar phrases to identify the message as a prophecy in their particular cultural setting. Their culture, however, was far removed from our own in the West. Though totally acceptable when used in Shakespeare's plays, such archaic language sounds odd in our context and it is, therefore, generally unhelpful.

- This sort of language suggests a high degree of certainty concerning the accuracy of contemporary prophecy. It also implies that this is the all-embracing and final word on the topic at hand. Paul, in contrast, suggested that a particular prophecy is likely to express just one aspect of a multi-faceted reality. His statement that 'we prophesy in part... Now I know in part' implies that our revelation is always limited in its scope (1 Corinthians 13:9 & 12).

- We should also note that many Old Testament prophecies did *not* start with the phrase 'thus saith the Lord' but were delivered in less formal, more straightforward ways. Some prophecy was a record of the prophet's dialogue with God. In the opening chapter of Habakkuk, the prophet lays his complaint before God, who responds to his interrogation. Habakkuk's prophecy did not need authenticating phrases to be taken seriously.

- Sometimes people use 'God told me' language out of a desire to be taken seriously, but its effect is to keep any feedback at bay; the content of a prophecy delivered with such certainty is difficult to challenge without appearing to be combative. Using phrases such as 'thus saith the Lord', or 'God has shown me' can place the speaker above contradiction and subverts the apostolic injunction for accountability. Preambles such as 'thus saith the Lord' or 'God told me' may be appropriate but only when we have a very high degree of certainty and even then our word needs to be offered to other mature believers to be weighed.

## Conversational Prophecy

Considering these different factors, prophecy today is often best delivered conversationally. If it is genuinely from God, it will be evident to those who truly desire to hear the voice of the Shepherd. Scripture tells us that his sheep know his voice (John 10:27). If it is God's voice, we will recognise it in the words and tone of what is spoken, without it having to be overtly brought to our attention.

Jesus appeared to favour conversational prophecy, as was evident in his meeting with the woman at the well (John 4). The interaction is almost playful and the revelation that she had had many husbands was communicated in the natural flow of conversation. Although we cannot know for sure the tone of his voice, it is highly likely that it was *not* communicated in a condemning manner – otherwise, she would have withdrawn then and there and have been reluctant for her friends to meet Jesus. It is important that our tone and choice of words reflect God's heart towards the recipient.

Many years ago, a friend felt he had a word from the Lord for the then Director General of the BBC (who was not a believer). He did not know how he was going to deliver it, but in the event, he went to a meeting about religious broadcasting with 300 other delegates from different walks of life. When my friend arrived, there was only one vacant seat left in the auditorium and, remarkably, it was right next to the Director General. My friend delivered the prophecy to him in a conversational style, avoiding any overtly religious language. I think this represents good practice - genuine prophecy is self-authenticating and, if he or she is open to God, the hearer will recognise its truth. We too can express prophetic revelation creatively and in a culturally appropriate way.

The next three chapters examine the range of gifts that fall under the rubric of prophecy. Related gifts include words of knowledge and wisdom, dreams and visions. These are all forms of revelation and, at times, they are difficult to distinguish from what is traditionally regarded as prophecy.

# 7

# Revealed Knowledge

There are instances in the Gospels where Jesus appeared to know something of importance about a person on first meeting them. At the end of the first chapter of John's Gospel, we read that Jesus encountered Nathanael and accurately described his character, telling him that he was scrupulously honest - without 'guile', or falsehood. He then went on to describe exactly what he was doing just before they met: 'Before Philip called you, *when you were under the fig tree*, I saw you.' Nathanael was amazed by this revelation and it convinced him that Jesus was indeed the Messiah (John 1:49). Jesus went on to predict that Nathanael would have a greater revelation of himself as the bridge between heaven and earth.

We see a similar dynamic in Jesus' encounter with the Samaritan woman at a well (John 4). The likely backstory was that she had been the victim of several husbands who had used her and then got rid of her (divorce for men was easy at that time). As we saw earlier, Jesus described her history of relationships with men in some detail and he did this conversationally, without resorting to any form of religious language. These two examples demonstrate how knowledge, based not on observation but on revelation, drew people to Jesus. Most Charismatics regard these stories as examples of what Paul meant by the phrase 'a word of knowledge':

> To each [person] is given the manifestation of the Spirit for the common good. To one is given ... *the utterance [word] of knowledge* according to the same Spirit...
> 1 CORINTHIANS 12:7-8

Phrases such as 'prophetic revelation' or 'receiving revealed knowledge' may actually be preferable ways to describe these examples as there is some debate among theologians concerning the exact meaning of the phrase 'word of knowledge'.[23]

Many Christians report instances of their having received revelation about another person or situation. I have a friend who was on holiday and engaged someone in conversation because he discerned certain things about her. He told her that she worked with children, had a major writing project in progress and that she was encountering problems in her relationship with her father. He is experienced in such things and these prophetic intuitions proved to be accurate. As a result of this interaction, she accompanied two people to a church service and became a Christian.

Some years ago, I led a small rural church. If somebody asked to see me to discuss an undisclosed issue I would pray before meeting them. Sometimes, a clear sense of the underlying issue would form in my mind, not based on logic or observation. I found that this was usually accurate and it helped focus our discussion on the most relevant topic. This kind of revealed knowledge concerning people and situations has been a common occurrence down the centuries. Here are two examples:

## George Fox

George Fox lived in the 17th century, a time of great political and social upheaval, involving the English Civil War. He is, perhaps, best known for his journal in which he recorded his most memorable and formative experiences. Fox realised that the lifestyle of many Christians was inconsistent with their profession of faith and as a result withdrew from organised religion. He had become disillusioned with churches which emphasised the Bible but left little room for actual experiences of the God of the Bible. He set out on a quest to know more of God, others joined him and eventually he founded a group that

---

[23] The phrase 'a word of knowledge' occurs only in this passage. In the rest of the letter, Paul uses the term 'knowledge' to describe an awareness of the nature of God (or in other instances, heretical secret knowledge). Some argue that it is, therefore, unlikely that he uses the term differently in chapter 12.

would later become the Quakers. Alongside a strong emphasis on scripture, George Fox held out the possibility of a direct encounter with Jesus.

His ministry was initiated by having had contact with a man called Brown:

> [Brown] had great prophecies and sights upon his death bed of me. He spoke only of what I should be made instrumental by the Lord to bring forth. And of others, he spoke that they should come to nothing; which was fulfilled on some who then were something in show. When this man was buried, a great work of the Lord fell upon me.
>
> GEORGE FOX'S JOURNAL

This 'great work of the Lord' included the reception of revelation from God. At times, he seemed to know how successful evangelistic efforts would be in specific villages. In his journal, he recounts being in one location and standing on a hill to survey the surrounding countryside. He told his companion, a Welsh Quaker called John ap John, 'in what places God would raise up a people to himself'. His predictions proved to be accurate and this experience was repeated in other places.

On another occasion, drawing near the city of Lichfield, he felt that God prompted him to remove his shoes before entering the city limits. As he walked through the city there appeared to him to be a channel of blood flowing through the streets and he began proclaiming, 'Woe to you bloody city of Lichfield'. Fox later learned that much blood had been shed in Lichfield over the centuries, including that of many Christians who had been martyred during the persecutions under Diocletian in the early 5th century.

Seven years before the plague swept through London, Fox had recorded in his journal a vision of the city lying in heaps, with its gates fallen. In 1665 the plague decimated the population and the following year the Fire of London destroyed over 13,000 homes. When he saw the city for himself, he recorded that what he saw was 'just as it had been represented to me' years earlier. His earlier vision had been fulfilled in great detail.

Fox's journal gives the impression that he was not at all easy to get along with. He was abrasive and prone to confronting people, but, despite these character flaws, he appears to have exhibited clear prophetic gifts, including that of receiving revealed knowledge.

## William Branham

The 1940s and '50s saw the beginning of the so-called Healing Revival in the USA. This involved prominent Pentecostal figures such as Oral Roberts, Jack Coe, T L Osborn and A A Allen. The Healing Revival was an evangelistic form of Pentecostalism and tent crusade meetings, large and small, swept through North America at this time.

William Branham was a part of this movement and he regularly exhibited the gift of receiving revealed knowledge throughout his ministry, although he became a controversial figure within Pentecostalism. He had received only a very basic education, and his personal life was tragic in the extreme, but despite these setbacks, he became a prominent healing evangelist.[24] He is reported to have had a remarkable healing ministry, but, towards the end of his life, not only promoted teachings which deviated from Christian orthodoxy but also insisted his followers should acknowledge him to be *the* end-time prophet.

Branham's one-time campaign manager, Ern Baxter, described his ministry of 'words of knowledge'. As people formed a line to be prayed for by Branham, Baxter would make a written note of people's symptoms and other details which he kept for his own use (not showing them to anyone). Branham would, without seeing Ern Baxter's notes, accurately describe their illnesses. He was also famed for revealing details of people's lives, such as their names and addresses, which he would not have known by natural means. He would reveal these details before he began to pray for them to raise their levels of faith. Baxter eventually parted company with Branham over some of his more extreme teachings but he was a reliable eyewitness to his ministry. There are several YouTube videos which show Branham in action.

---

[24] For further details see: David Harrell, *All Things Are Possible: The Healing & Charismatic Revivals in Modern America*. (Bloomington: Indiana University Press 1975), 27-40.

As well as critiquing the more negative aspects of the ministries concerned, it is important, nonetheless, to learn from them.

## The Value of Revealed Knowledge

Jesus received and communicated revealed knowledge as part of his ministry. This gift communicates an awareness that God knows us intimately and can lead us into a deeper relationship with him, as is evident in the stories of Nathanael and the woman at the well. At times, he was aware of people's unspoken attitude towards him (John 2:24; Matthew 9:4). Isaiah prophesied that the Messiah would have 'the Spirit of knowledge' (Isaiah 11:2) and we also, as the body of Christ, need this gift to fulfil our ministry to one another and to the world around us.

A now-departed friend with a wide ministry is reported to have often sought God for revealed knowledge. When he had a speaking engagement, he would pray beforehand that God would give him the name of someone God wanted him either to meet, prophesy over or pray for. The person would be unknown to him but as he called out the name publicly, on many, many occasions it proved to be correct. The experience of knowing that God wants to communicate to you personally, having one's name highlighted in this way, can be very affirming.

This gift can be actively sought, although it is possible that we receive such gifts of knowledge more often than we realise. It can, in fact, be difficult to recognise as such because it often feels quite natural. But as we share our intuitions and check whether or not they are accurate we can grow and develop in this gift.

## The Importance of Character

Gifted people often get away with their faults because we fail to treat them as we would any other person. The accounts in this chapter illustrate that heroes always have feet of clay. George Fox held views that might be regarded today as sectarian. He certainly could have done with being discipled in his use of abrasive language and could have been helped to see others' points of view.

William Branham started well and, sadly, ended in deception but, without seeking to excuse him, there were factors which may well have been involved that are often overlooked. He had a traumatic background with multiple bereavements, added to which his great compassion resulted in an incredibly punishing unsustainable workload, as he sought to help as many people as possible. It may be the case that his traumatic early experiences as well as fostering compassion for others left him with a dysfunctional drive to overcompensate. Today we might regard the aberrations of his later years as being the result of a breakdown.

In more recent times, the stories of some of the so-called Kansas City Prophets illustrate how giftedness is not a guard against sin or deception. Their stories highlight that prominent figures in the Christian world, including, or especially, those who exercise spectacular gifts, need to grow in the fruit of the Spirit and need to have forums for accountability.

It would be a mistake to lay all the blame for the errors of those with such remarkable gifts at their feet alone. Major problems ensue once we, the Church, place ministers on a pedestal, as they are bound to fall off at some point. Idealisation is often followed by denigration once we realise our heroes also have feet of clay.

*We ourselves become culpable whenever we allow gifted leaders to be elevated above contradiction or challenge.* This is relevant today if apostolic and prophetic ministers are promoted as a form of super-elite Christian, without the need for normal checks and balances. Accountability to a congregation, the recognition of our limitations and the exercise of humility are essential components of healthy church systems.

## Gifted People Need Pastoral Care

The Church often fails to exercise due care for those with extraordinary gifts. We are, of course, aware of the stories of those who reap large monetary rewards from their ministry and the fact that these people have used their abilities to accrue wealth can make us wary of others who appear to have prophetic or other gifts. But at the same time, many gifted people are poorly cared for by the Church.

Sometimes gifted people are assumed to be a different breed who transcend the need for rest, relaxation, friendship and good advice. The story of Simon Peter in the New Testament (or David in the Old) reminds us that prominent leaders are no different from other people. They, like us, are fallible, however clear their call from God and however zealous or well-intentioned they may be.

Gifted people need both friends and peer-level relationships, those who will ensure that the need for times of withdrawal and rest is not overlooked. The story of William Branham is clearly a cautionary tale, but it is also the tale of a wounded man who was idealised by his followers. He was subjected to huge pressure with so many in need of God's healing touch. Unlike Mother Theresa, Branham came from a Christian tradition with little emphasis on the need to develop a rhythm of prayer and the importance of structures that can be called upon to provide support, advice or correction in times of need.

# 8

# A Word of Wisdom

Wisdom is of utmost importance as it enables us, individually and as churches, to be more fruitful. Wisdom is so fundamental that Proverbs paints the most beautiful and profound picture of wisdom being alongside God when he began his work of creation, long before he made anything else (Proverbs 8:22-31). Although at times, some Charismatics may attach a lower value to wisdom than to prophecy or other forms of revealed knowledge, wisdom cannot actually be regarded highly enough - Jesus himself is identified by biblical texts as being the embodiment of God's wisdom (1 Corinthians 1:24).

*A word of wisdom* is a spiritual gift - it is the fact that the Holy Spirit is the source of wisdom that distinguishes it from wisdom acquired solely through reflection on experience.

## A Missed Opportunity

The huge popularity of Jordan Peterson's book *Twelve Rules for Life* illustrates the fact that many of us, whether or not we have a faith, desire to have greater wisdom than we currently possess. People are concerned with issues such as how to successfully navigate relationships, how to create balance in busy lives, how to deal with those who oppose us and so on.

Zen Buddhism has stolen a march on Christianity, having cornered the market on religious wisdom! In the popular view, wisdom is found in the pithy sayings of the Zen masters rather than in anything we in the Church have to offer. Zen wisdom ranges from esoteric questions designed to make us think such as, 'Can you hear the sound of one hand clapping?' to more straightforward statements such as, 'Wise men don't seek to judge – they seek to understand'. We in the Church are often reticent when it comes to sharing the wisdom we have to offer – or alternatively we offer it in overly forceful, and therefore unattractive, ways.

We actually have several sources of wisdom at our disposal: the wisdom contained in the Bible, the written wisdom of the Church through the ages and more immediately-inspired wisdom imparted by the Spirit today. Christian wisdom is often an untapped resource.

During a car journey with an unchurched friend, we were discussing the difficult dynamics operating in a group of people with whom we were involved. I quoted a short aphorism which impressed him and he commented that I was full of wisdom. I had to admit that the saying wasn't original – it was actually something Jesus had said – but my friend could see that it was a wise way to approach a tricky situation.

The best description of wisdom that I have come across is 'instruction in the art of living'. Again, the phrase 'the art of living' is not associated in the popular mind with Christianity, as it is more likely to be used by New Age organisations to promote eastern mysticism. But living is an art and we are not left to find our own way in life.

## A Broad View of Wisdom

> To each [person] is given the manifestation of the Spirit for the common good. To one is given ... the utterance [word] of wisdom.
> 1 CORINTHIANS 12:7-8

It is commonly agreed that the phrase 'a word of wisdom' includes those instances when we receive divine wisdom to resolve a seemingly unresolvable situation at a particular point in time. Books on spiritual gifts frequently cite the example of Solomon when he was faced with two mothers who each claimed that the same baby was their own (1 Kings 3:16-28). He had the God-inspired idea to command that the baby be divided in two and one half given to each mother. This would have resulted in the death of the baby and the genuine mother was identified by the fact that she was willing to give up all claim to her offspring to ensure his survival. This is an example of the wisdom that God can give us when we find ourselves in challenging circumstances.

But many commentators, Charismatic and otherwise, suggest we should adopt a much broader understanding of the phrase 'a word of wisdom' to include any action inspired by the Spirit that is related to the art of living or to speaking wisely. This includes the wisdom expressed in books or conversations, the ability to respond insightfully to our opponents, as well as the teaching of practical Christian living. Catholics may also consider some advice given in formal contexts of spiritual direction as being words of wisdom.

Revelation may, of course, draw on our experience and can be a succinct summary of what we have learned, but it always goes beyond being merely the exercise of intellect. The determining factor is whether wisdom is *purely* an expression of human reason or whether it is wisdom 'from above', a gift of the Holy Spirit. Adopting a broad understanding of the nature of a word of wisdom helps us to pay close attention to wisdom as communicated in different guises.

## Paul's Use of the Term 'Wisdom'

As in the case of the phrase 'word of knowledge', 1 Corinthians 12 is the only place in the Bible where 'word of wisdom' is used. We need, therefore, to appreciate the background to Paul's use of the term wisdom. In 1 Corinthians 1:18-2:16, he referred to the wisdom of the world and contrasted this with the 'foolishness' of the Cross. He went on to explain that Jesus embodied true wisdom, the wisdom of God. God's wisdom, as evidenced in Christ's willingness to embrace weakness, contrasts with human wisdom, which emphasises the power of might.

Having established this contrast between human wisdom and the wisdom of God, Paul then described the way in which he taught true wisdom to mature Christians:

> Yet among the mature *we do impart wisdom*... a secret and hidden wisdom of God, which God decreed before the ages for our glory...
> Now we have received not the spirit of the world, but the Spirit

who is from God, *that we might understand the things freely given us by God*. And we impart this in *words* not taught by human wisdom but *taught by the Spirit*, interpreting spiritual truth to those who are spiritual.
1 CORINTHIANS 2:6-7 & 12-13

Paul clearly regarded wisdom as crucial and emphasised that the source of all wisdom is the Spirit – wisdom, in other words, is a spiritual gift. It is likely that this is what Paul had in mind when he wrote about 'a word of wisdom' in chapter 12. This is not the wisdom of how best to invest in the stock market or how to win friends and influence people – it includes the wisdom of embracing our vulnerability and being wholly dependent on God, just as Jesus was. This makes it likely that Paul would have understood 'a word of wisdom' as the communication of God-given revelation, inspired by the Spirit, that encapsulated true wisdom for living.

## The Wisdom of the Desert

The so-called Desert Fathers are an example of a movement that placed a very high value on wisdom. Beginning in the third century, Egyptian men and women sought to escape the ensnaring lure of a society that, although superficially 'Christianised', represented compromise and the absence of true zeal. In withdrawing to the desert they experienced solitude, silence and simplicity of lifestyle. St Anthony is perhaps the best-known of these early monks. Those who followed in his wake are known as the Desert Fathers, with their female counterparts, the Desert Mothers.

Anthony initially lived on the edge of society but later he withdrew deeper and deeper into the desert. We might think that this would limit his effectiveness, but this was not the case. He was actively sought out by both ordinary people and the ruling classes for his advice. He was also attributed with possessing healing gifts.

The route to spiritual formation taken by Anthony and others proved to be highly attractive. By the time of Anthony's death, there were an estimated 5,000 monks in the desert and many of these sought the advice of older and wiser monks to instruct them in the art of living simply and of seeking God's presence. Small communities grew up and eventually larger monastic communities emerged under the leadership of figures such as Pachomius. Pachomius was attributed with prophetic abilities and is said to have prayed in tongues and worked miracles. The Desert Fathers were renowned for their memorable wise sayings, many of which were collected by John Cassian, a monk from present-day Romania. His book, *The Conferences of the Desert Fathers*, was widely influential and it helped shape many of the subsequent monastic movements including Celtic monasticism. Many of the sayings in the stories of the desert monks contained a degree of wry humour.

One of my favourite sayings was given by Abbot Moses. A young monk came to him and asked him for a word. His reply was, 'Go, sit in your cell, and your cell will teach you everything'. Presumably, the young monk was looking for profound teaching or perhaps he was seeking 'the secret of spiritual success'. This is an age-old quest and we see it today in many books that promise to provide us with the missing ingredient to supercharge our individual lives or our churches.

Abbot Moses was much wiser than to provide this young man with a superficial answer and, rather than suggesting a quick fix, he sent him back to the mundane reality of work and prayer in the narrow confines of his everyday life. The wise abbot realised that God uses the circumstances in which we find ourselves, with their profound limitations, to mould us. It is only by embracing the ordinary that we are shaped into people with a grounded approach to life and spirituality. Abbot Moses was clearly very astute as he identified the temptation to run away from the very circumstances that God has allowed for our growth.

A recent example of this sort of pithy saying comes from a more recent monastic source, Thomas Merton. He wrote, 'In order to become myself I must cease to be what I always thought I wanted to be'. This saying has been very helpful to me personally and it is written in a section of my journal that is reserved for wise quotations. It reminds me not to compare myself with others whose gifts I greatly admire. It is easy for us to wish to be someone other than ourselves. In doing so we can neglect the person who God has actually made us to be. These succinct sayings encapsulate profound wisdom. They are words of wisdom that can save us from being ensnared by our enduring neuroses.

There are several examples of words of wisdom recorded in the Bible. This includes immediately-inspired wisdom that was operative in the example of Solomon and the two women. Here are a few examples of different sorts of words of wisdom:

## Wisdom to resolve conflict

The early church in Acts was faced with a situation in which Greek widows complained that, compared to the Hebrew widows, they were being treated unfairly in the daily distribution of food. This is the sort of conflict that arises when one group feels it is at a disadvantage because of, for example, their ethnicity, gender or other identifiable characteristic. The apostles came up with the solution of asking the whole church to select a specific group of people to distribute the food. This course of action was an expression of wisdom and the fact that it 'pleased the whole gathering' demonstrates how very wise it was (Acts 6:1-7). As pointed out previously, the distribution of food required planning and administration.

## Wisdom to confront our opponents

The next story in Acts describes Stephen being challenged by men from one particular synagogue who objected to his teaching. It is recorded that his opponents 'could not withstand *the wisdom and the Spirit* with which he was speaking' (Acts 6:10). Wisdom was clearly in evidence in the young church, operative both in decision-making and in extempore speech.

## Wisdom for ethical or religious dilemmas

One dilemma that faced the apostles is described in great detail in Acts 15. The conversion of a large number of Gentiles raised the issue of whether or not they needed to be circumcised. There were strong feelings on both sides of the argument. Their decision was recorded in a letter sent to the churches outlining the divine wisdom that they had received in the course of their debate. A word of wisdom had emerged through a process of dialogue:

> For it has seemed good *to the Holy Spirit and us* to lay on you no greater burden than these requirements…
> ACTS 15:28

The Holy Spirit can impart wisdom to those who lead churches when they need to respond to ethical or religious dilemmas, including those involving wider societal issues. Knowing how to uphold biblical principles in the context of love, so that justice and mercy might meet, is not always straightforward and may require God's wisdom.

In addition to these practical examples of wisdom being imparted to the early church, there are also large portions of scripture which are described as 'wisdom literature'. The fact that they have been included in the Bible means that these 'words of wisdom' were regarded as having been inspired by the Holy Spirit.

## Wisdom Literature

A significant portion of the Old Testament comes under the heading of wisdom literature. This includes books that contain straightforward instruction, such as Proverbs, as well as narratives such as Job, Ruth and Esther. Ecclesiastes is yet another example of wisdom literature, more akin to philosophical discussion. Some Psalms are also included under the umbrella of wisdom literature (see Psalms 1 and 49) and several of these songs and poems describe conversations with God where a change of heart occurs because wisdom has been imparted in the course of dialogue.

We should note that in some of these examples 'wisdom' is a prompt to think through the issues, a guide to what is important rather than providing a set of ready-made answers and much of the teaching of Jesus follows this pattern. He sometimes simply asked the most penetrating question, making his hearers think, rather than actually providing the solution himself.

The teachings of Jesus contain much practical wisdom appropriate to the setting of first-century Israel, such as how to respond when asked to carry a Roman soldier's backpack for one mile (Matthew 5:41). He communicated this in a variety of ways using pithy sayings, telling stories, parables, humour and hyperbole (i.e. he taught by exaggerating certain things!) Most of his teaching focused on the practicalities of life. The Sermon on the Mount, commonly regarded as a reframing of the Law in the Old Testament, is a form of wisdom literature. The Beatitudes (Matthew 5:1-11) could be the basis for a self-help book today, entitled 'How to Live Happy' (blessed).

The book of James is thoroughly grounded in the wisdom tradition of the Old Testament. Following the example of Proverbs, wisdom for James was very practical. He emphasised right living (orthopraxy) to the extent that Martin Luther thought he downplayed grace in favour of works. According to Luther the letter of James was not worthy of inclusion in the New Testament!

Early on in his letter, James tells us that if we lack wisdom, we should ask God and that it will be given to us generously (James 1:5-7). He sees a word of wisdom as something that is *promised* to us, emerging from our dialogue with God. He later goes on to describe the contrast between divine wisdom and a more pragmatic worldly wisdom:

> But the wisdom from above is first pure, then peaceable, gentle, open to reason, full of mercy and good fruits, impartial and sincere.
> JAMES 3:17

In charismatic circles, it is not uncommon to find people claiming that they know the will of God and stating this with a degree of conviction that does not allow for discussion. Paradoxically, this automatically signals that it is unlikely to be of divine origin as revelation 'from above' is open to reason and is not an expression of a personal or hidden agenda. The fact that we believe that God has shown us something does not mean that we can then subvert the normal process of openness and accountability.

## Immediate Inspiration or a Process?

I have mentioned that in the Charismatic Movement a word of wisdom is commonly regarded as an in-the-moment-inspired word but some of the examples cited suggest a broader understanding (especially of the time scale involved). My impression is that many of the sayings of the Desert Fathers, inspired by the Holy Spirit, would at times have resulted from a process of discernment that drew on entire life experience. The Spirit can take these experiences, along with what we have learned in our walk with God, and distil them into memorable phrases that can help us and others to live wisely.

The Holy Spirit also helps us with timing so that, rather than casting our pearls before swine, we know when the recipient is open to receiving any wisdom. He leads us to share our hard-won wisdom with particular people at particular times rather than wasting our words on those who are not yet ready.

An example of the ability to communicate wisdom was evident in the ministry of one of the leading founders of the British New Church Movement, Gerald Coates. As part of being himself and a memorable and colourful figure, he produced some extremely memorable sayings. My wife and I heard many of these sayings 40 years ago and can still recall them to this day. He succinctly described attitudes that destroy our fellowship with one another as being 'hidden suspicion and vested interest'. Another highly memorable phrase of Gerald's was 'your ministry is probably what you like doing!' Of course, this is not always the case, but it helped correct the idea prevalent at the time that God was likely to call us to do things that we would find arduous and unfulfilling.

In this chapter, I have argued that a word of wisdom can be imparted at a particular time of need or it can emerge more gradually through a process of Spirit-guided reflection and discernment. We might even regard much of Paul's pastoral advice, such as is found in 1 Corinthians, as being words of wisdom. Broadening our understanding of this gift is important as Charismatics need to see that wisdom, received either in an instant or more gradually over a period of time, originates from the activity of the Holy Spirit and, as such, needs to be taken very seriously. Wisdom is absolutely crucial and should never be regarded as being less desirable or less important than prophecy, which, as scripture tells us, 'one day' will pass away.

9

# Dreams & Visions

In the Bible, we see that God frequently communicated through dreams and visions. Personally, I have had very few dreams which I have felt were from God but my most significant dream occurred in 1987. At the time I was working in a challenging medical practice located in the centre of a social housing development and, a year before I had the dream, we had planted a church in the village where we were living.

I have always found it easier when I can concentrate on just one role and combining medicine with church leadership was challenging - in addition, we had three young children, so life was quite pressured. I had a strong desire to focus either on church leadership or on medical practice, but I did not want to take my fate into my own hands and miss God's will for my life. The way forward was not easy to discern.

One night, however, I had a dream in which I was on board an aeroplane flight and the plane had stopped temporarily in an Indian city. As I descended from the plane two people caught my attention. The first was an American businessman, smartly dressed and very wealthy. The second was a female missionary, living a sacrificial life as evidenced by her poor clothing, though her lifestyle was actually attractive to me (I have never been terribly fashion-conscious!) I felt conflicted and wanted to make this a permanent stop and follow one or the other into the city. On waking, I realised that what I should do in the dream was to get back on the aeroplane and not make this the permanent stopping-off point.

The meaning of the dream and how it applied to my circumstances were clear to me. I had to stay on my existing course. I should not go with the businessman, who symbolised the pursuit of financial security, nor should I go with the missionary, who represented a life given purely to Christian ministry.[25] I needed to get back on the plane and continue my existing journey. Furthermore, the symbolism was interesting because I realised that one day the plane would actually land. The arrangement at that time was not permanent, which was reassuring, but it was the journey I needed to pursue.

In retrospect, I can see that my remaining in medicine provided certain learning experiences that helped me in my future ministry. I also needed to retain a role in church leadership and continue to nurture the newly planted church. I could easily have opted for either course, but I believe that had I done so at that particular time, much would have been lost. The dream was a powerful influence in convincing me that I should not make any sudden changes and it confirmed what my wife had been telling me for some time!

## Saint Patrick

The dreams and visions of Saint Patrick, sometimes known as The Apostle to the Irish, are well documented. Patrick lived in the 5th century and we have two documents written by Patrick's own hand. These texts have always been considered to be authentic which makes his first-hand testimony all the more compelling. In addition, he wrote with much humility which gives added credibility to his account of his mission to Ireland.

Patrick was not, in fact, the first missionary to Ireland as Palladius had exercised the ministry of a bishop in the South, albeit with limited success. Patrick was British but was abducted at the age of 16 and taken as a slave to work as a shepherd on the west coast of Ireland. Although raised in a Christian home, he had no active faith until his captivity when he began to pray earnestly to God. His escape from slavery was triggered by a series of dreams from God pinpointing a port 200 miles away and identifying a particular boat that would take him back across the Irish Sea.

---

[25] I am not suggesting that to be in medicine is to pursue affluence. It was more a case that switching to medicine full-time, though challenging, represented financial security.

Having returned home he had a further dream, or possibly a vision, in which he heard the voice of those on the west coast of Ireland calling to him: 'We ask you Holy Boy to come and walk among us again'. On returning to Ireland, he faced much opposition. He recorded another dream in which he saw his own face being denigrated by others but went on to hear the voice of God supporting him against those who opposed him. This experience gave him great confidence, assuring him that he was innocent of all accusations against him.

Patrick had great success and it is said that he converted 40 of the 150 Irish tribes to the new Christian faith. Secular historians tend to attribute his achievements to his personal charisma combined with the fact that he brought the gift of writing to Ireland, something which was much coveted by the ruling classes. His own account suggests that his achievements had much more to do with the power of God made evident in confronting the forces of paganism.

However we understand the success of his ministry, and I personally believe that it involved the exercise of spiritual gifts, it is undeniable that dreams and visions played a crucial role at various turning points in his life. In fact, according to Patrick's own account dreams and visions were the most common way in which God communicated to him.

## Dreams & Visions in the Bible

> I will pour out my Spirit on all flesh,
> and your sons and your daughters shall prophesy,
> and your young men shall see visions,
> and your old men shall dream dreams...
> ACTS 2:17

Peter quoted this passage from Joel to explain to his hearers the significance of the events they witnessed on the day of Pentecost. Peter appears to have viewed dreams and visions as normative. The outpouring of the Spirit was intended for both men and women, 'your sons and daughters', and the young men/old men language is likely to be inclusive of both sexes.

Some people read significance into the fact that it is young men who see visions and old men who dream dreams. In other words, the dreams of old men relate to the past recaptured in their dreams. The problem with this view is that dreams in the Bible usually relate to the present and future, rather than to the past. Joel was simply using what is called parallelism, a common device in Hebrew literature where the same point was made in several different ways for emphasis – in this case, to emphasise that the pouring out of God's Spirit would include all mankind, irrespective of age or other defining factors.

Prophecy, visions and dreams are treated equally and considered as one in this passage. It is debatable, in fact, whether there is any difference inherent in the nature of dreams and visions. They are actually one and the same thing and dreams are sometimes referred to in the Bible as being 'visions of the night' (Genesis 46:2).

Jeffrey Kranz has helpfully listed the dreams recorded in scripture and here are some of his findings:[26]

- There are 21 dreams recorded in the Bible
- 10 of these are in Genesis, 6 in Matthew's Gospel and 3 in Daniel
- 5 of these dreams surround the birth of Christ

In addition, it is notable that 11 out of 21 dreams are received by those who are not descendants of Israel, God's chosen people. This includes King Abimelech, Pharoah and his servants, Nebuchadnezzar and Pilate's wife (Genesis 20, 40, 47; Daniel 2 and 4; Matthew 27:19).

## Distinguishing Between Direction and Symbolism

Some dreams and visions contain simple instructions to pursue a certain course of action - while others employ symbols and visual imagery to convey truth, rather than more literal descriptive language. Visions are more frequently recorded than dreams, particularly in the writings of the Old Testament prophets and in Revelation. Many of the writings of the prophets evoke strong symbolic imagery, for example when the image of the coming of a thunderstorm was portrayed by Habakkuk (3:3-4), and it is reasonable to assume that much of what

---

[26] https://overviewbible.com/infographic-dreams-bible/

was written represented a description of actual visions received.

Clearly, dreams containing specific direction are more straightforward to interpret than those without, even if they are not actually easy to carry out! Perhaps the clearest example is God's instruction to Joseph that he should marry Mary and, later, that they should flee to and return from Egypt (Matthew 1:18-2:23). While we need to discern that any dream is actually from God rather than from our psyche, the meaning of this sort of dream is usually quite straightforward.

When it comes to dreams and visions that are more symbolic in nature their interpretation requires further insight from God. We can see this in evidence in several Old Testament passages. Genesis 40 recounts the story of two of Pharaoh's household servants who each had a symbolic dream that neither of them could understand. The interpretation of these dreams was unclear until it was revealed to Jacob's son Joseph.

Although it is not listed as a spiritual gift in 1 Corinthians 12, it would seem that dream interpretation has some parallels with interpreting speaking in tongues. Both concern the interpretation of a language that is normally much less accessible to us naturally. Dream interpretation, like the interpretation of tongues, requires acute levels of discernment to pick up the associated mood and tone. Without this gift, the meaning of a dream or vision can be unintelligible. It is to the interpretation of symbolic language that we now turn. There follows suggested principles we might employ to understand the symbolism used in dreams and visions:

## Be Aware that Symbols are Culture-Specific

Much of what we read in the prophetic books of the Bible would have been more easily understood by the original readers than by us. It has been suggested that some of the symbolic language employed by John in Revelation was an attempt to conceal the true meaning of his writing from the authorities whilst at the same time revealing things that would be plainly understood by his audience. For example, the beast from the sea in Revelation 13 would have been identified with the cult of the divine emperor, which was imported to Asia Minor from across the sea in Rome. This is a complex topic, well beyond the scope of this book, but perhaps the most important point for us to be aware of is that *we need to interpret symbols in the light of how they were likely to have been understood in their original cultural setting.*

Jesus frequently employed images and scenes from everyday life in his teaching. His hearers could easily relate to what he said as it connected with their culture and their daily existence. We and others may need help to understand such specific contexts to appreciate what is meant. Jesus communicated his care for the people of Israel by using the highly symbolic imagery of being a shepherd while today, the Inuit, for example, although having experience of caring for packs of huskies, will themselves have little or no experience of shepherding flocks of sheep and may consequently need to do some research.

The likelihood is that God communicates using symbols that we as the hearers can relate to in terms of our culture and personal experience. Imagine, for example, that someone has a dream involving a lion. If that particular person lives in an African village, the image might conjure up a sense of danger. Yet, that same image of a lion, if dreamt of by an English football team supporter, might arouse feelings of patriotism and memories of the 1966 World Cup rather than of fear. The Church, however, might immediately take courage from that same image with thoughts of Jesus, as the Lion of the Tribe of Judah. This crucial need for awareness of what specific symbols might suggest in a particular time and context brings us to the next topic.

## Use Dream Lexicons Sparingly

I have a book on dream interpretation by John Paul Jackson called *20 Top Dreams* in which the author seeks to interpret common symbols in dreams. He wisely emphasises the need to rely on the Holy Spirit for interpretation and to take into account personal and cultural factors to determine the significance of particular symbols. He draws on his own wide experience in dream interpretation to look at commonly occurring themes. In his experience, dreams involving transport (such as cars, trains or planes) are often intended to guide us in our ministry. This does, in fact, seem to have been the case in the personal example recounted at the beginning of this chapter.

It is not unreasonable to conclude that common, perhaps archetypal, symbols occur time and time again in our dreams and visions. A common example is a dream involving sitting an exam without having done the necessary preparation. It often represents feeling unprepared in some area of life and would generally have a psychological origin, but Jackson suggests that, alternatively, it might indicate that we need to learn something which we failed to learn earlier in life. I am unsure as to how we can test this idea apart from in individual instances where we may sense that this interpretation is a good fit with our current circumstances.

Personally, I have tended to shy away from approaches which suggest particular symbols have universal meanings. When I worked as a psychotherapist I would often listen to accounts of my clients' dreams. I would usually not interpret them immediately and sometimes a probable meaning would emerge during the course of a session. Some of these dreams appeared almost to be parables commenting on a client's situation and representing in coded ways their dilemmas and possible ways forward.

## Consider the Possible Sources of Dreams and Visions

I will not comment in depth on the relationship between visual and auditory hallucinations and physical or mental illness other than to say simply that this relationship does exist. Certain forms of epilepsy, for example, at particular times can produce the sensation of smell in the sufferer. These are very real experiences and, although they account for a small minority of dreams and visions, we should be aware that they exist. In addition to these less common causes there are other possible sources for visions and dreams including psychological sources when our unconscious mind seeks to resolve internal conflicts and also that of spiritual attack intending to discourage, disturb or intimidate us. This brings us to the topic of discerning the source of revelation and weighing prophecy, but first we will consider how local churches can be conducive to the exercise of prophetic gifts.

# 10

# Creating a Culture for Prophecy

The local church is the forum in which prophecy most often will be practised and where it is nurtured in individuals. Alongside having a theological commitment to prophecy, one very important factor is whether or not the culture created in a church is actually conducive to prophecy being given and received.

The word 'culture' refers to the atmosphere and environment created by both the leadership and the members of a congregation. Culture in this sense has been described as being 'the way we do things around here'. There are some church cultures which are conducive to the practice of prophecy and others that are not. When I think of particular churches, I would say that they fall into five categories:

- A controlling culture
- An overly permissive culture
- A blame culture
- A training culture
- A learning culture

Some of these cultures may co-exist, such as a controlling and a blame culture, whereas a learning culture and a blame culture are mutually exclusive. This is an important topic because prophecy will, I believe, only really thrive in a learning culture. Furthermore, a learning culture fits well with Paul's directive in 1 Corinthians to allow several people to prophesy and then discuss (weigh) what is said.

## A Controlling Culture

Sadly, in my experience, this is not uncommon in churches. Churches with a controlling culture often feel unwelcoming to new people, who are perceived as a threat by those in control. Often a leader, a family or a cabal will assume ownership of the church and any attempt others make to change things will effectively be resisted, either by the overt exercise of power or through more subtle means. I know of one church where the new minister decided a wall needed painting. Once this had been completed, a faction in the church forced him to repaint it in its original colour. There was no doubt as to where the real power lay.

Control is usually exercised in order to prevent change, which is perceived negatively unless initiated by the controlling faction. In such a culture prophecy is either unwelcome, as it can be disruptive to the status quo, or is permitted only when given by particular individuals.

## An Overly Permissive Culture

While a permission-giving culture is desirable, an overly-permissive culture is actually detrimental. In some settings, there is an unhelpful conspiracy of silence where more dubious prophecies simply pass without comment, in the hope that those present will simply have forgotten them by the next day. In the longer term, the failure to discuss prophetic words openly and honestly will erode the credibility of prophecy in a church and will deny the person concerned an opportunity to learn more and grow in the exercise of their gift.

A permissive culture can be motivated by the understandable desire to avoid any possible awkwardness and to protect the feelings of the person prophesying. Alternatively, it may be that a church is so overawed by someone's ministry that, ignoring the scriptural injunction to test all things, their words are automatically assumed to be genuine prophecy. If we are overly deferent to those who claim to have had revelation, we are likely to fall prey to being misled. Ensuring that we have processes for discernment is vital, as we need to have ways to separate the good from the less good.

Paul countered a laissez-faire attitude where everything shared under the guise of prophecy is regarded as being from God: 'Do not despise prophecies, *but test everything*; hold fast that which is good'

(1 Thessalonians 5:20-21). This verse suggests that not every prophetic word is 'good' (genuine) and if we fail to test prophecy, we may eventually end up despising it.

## A Blame Culture

A blame culture is another way of exercising control through disapproval. Anyone who risks doing something new is likely to make mistakes along the way. Rather than mistakes being seen as part of the learning process, even as good learning experiences, they are regarded as being transgressions requiring the person concerned to be called to account. In this sort of culture, prophecies will be subject to criticism, rather than weighed, and woe betide those whose prophecies are found wanting in some area.

## A Training Culture

A training culture is one in which certain people are encouraged to undergo an authorised course of training to credential them for a particular activity, such as leading worship, pastoral care or lay preaching. A training culture is positive in that it enables a proportion of people to play a part in the ministry of the church. This is a better environment for prophecy than the cultures we have examined so far, but is still unlikely to see prophecy widely in operation.

Such training aims to produce a standardised 'product', which is good in that it prevents wildly inappropriate or unskilled contributions to the life of the church. The downside of a training culture includes the fact that it promotes a one-size-fits-all approach to church gatherings (and to the life of the church in general) and the ministry that results is likely to lack diversity. Another difficulty is that it creates a culture where people can only take part if they have been trained and this excludes many gifted people.

Certain forms of ministry, particularly in the established churches, require being credentialled, as is seen in denominations which require a clergyperson to be the celebrant at Communion. Yet even in such churches, there can still be scope for wide participation in certain settings, such as in small groups, where Paul's vision that the saints (i.e. all believers) will 'do the work of ministry' can be realised (Ephesians 4:12). This brings us to the final culture under consideration:

## A Learning Culture

Leadership roles in the Church exist to enable and facilitate each one of us to contribute positively to the life of the people of God (Ephesians 4:1-16). This is not simply a case of church leaders imparting information through biblical teaching or providing pastoral support in times of need; Paul views the local church, including its leadership, as having a crucial role in the development and growth of each person's ministry. We learn as we practise our gifts and serve an apprenticeship in the Spirit under the guidance of others. In addition to the role of leadership, every member plays a part in helping others grow in the gifts and fruit of the Spirit (Colossians 3:16).

Perhaps the first thing to stress is that such a culture has more to do with the 'feel' of a church than with specific protocols or rules. In fact, protocols, whether formal or informal, will naturally emerge from the particular culture of a church, whether a learning or a controlling culture, etc. This means that culture will often be implicit rather than stated outright (although at times it may need to be articulated).

A learning culture is one in which many people contribute to a gathering and it is accepted that others may comment on what is said. In our own setting, for example, we often facilitate a discussion after a talk has been given. Sometimes people will affirm what has been shared but at other times a different view may be expressed. This rarely ever causes offence but is broadening and thought-provoking. It is a culture, based on openness and trust, which is implicit rather than explicit. In terms of the practice of prophecy, to have a learning culture implies that others may comment on what has been shared and further prophetic words may be given. Although informal and unstructured, it is, I suspect, what Paul was describing in his protocol for prophecy in 1 Corinthians. This process is not heavy (discussion is not the same as blame) but neither is it permissive in terms of anything goes.

A learning culture develops slowly and it seems to me that developing such a culture is a task of leadership. It recognises that individual Christians are at different points on the learning curve regarding the exercise of prophetic gifts. We are all encouraged to earnestly desire prophecy and while many will be in the early stages of learning how to prophesy, others will be more experienced. We may be apprentices in the exercise of prophecy, just beginning our journey, or we may have developed to the extent that we have become master craftsmen through practice and experience.

Feedback and advice are particularly valuable when people are in the early stages of learning to prophesy as this accelerates growth in using the gift. Our ability to communicate what we sense in our spirit varies but however skilful we may be, there is always room for further learning and refinement. We are *all* disciples.

## Humility

The root of the word 'disciple' is learner (in the sense of being an apprentice) and Jesus commanded the Apostles to make learners in every nation (Matthew 28:18-20). As Scott McKnight points out in his book *The Kingdom Conspiracy*, we have often replaced the command to make disciples with getting people to make 'a decision'.

It is not difficult to create a learning culture once people realise that discipleship is crucial and that it is a lifelong process. Growing as followers of Jesus involves gaining understanding, putting understanding into practice, having feedback and either continuing in what we have learned or making further adjustments. This is only possible where humility is highly valued so that there is a willingness to receive feedback. The ability to give and receive feedback are skills that need to be understood and developed in churches.

A feedback culture can dissuade those who want to operate independently and can act as a safety net for others. In a previous church, I was approached by someone who was new to the church and wished to preach. I was uncertain as to whether this person was gifted or simply keen to promote himself but, on the other hand, I did not want to discourage him. I told him that he was welcome to preach and that when anyone did so, other people were free to respond to what was said and that there might be comments on it (I was explaining that we operated a learning culture). He never asked to speak again, and I suspect his desire to preach was based on a need to be beyond contradiction. A learning culture is very effective when people really want to hone their skills in a particular area based on a genuine desire to serve God - it does not pander to those who are primarily seeking acclamation or praise.

## Be Supportive

Especially in the early days of prophesying, we are likely to lack confidence and be prone to making elementary mistakes. We need to be careful to nurture people rather than discourage them as they take their first steps. When children learn to draw, for example, we do harm if we criticise them for colouring a face blue. We recognise that certain mistakes are age and stage-appropriate (or, alternatively, that they are following in the footsteps of Picasso!)

Open discussion, acknowledging the positive features of a prophecy, will help people develop. Occasional gentle feedback on any less-than-positive aspects will mitigate any long-term harmful effects. We might, for instance, help someone to change their style if they prophesy in a tactless or patronising manner which is more damaging than helpful.

In order to encourage people to share what they sense, it is sometimes necessary to provide them with validation as many people lack confidence. At times, I have been aware that God has given someone else in the room a prophetic message or a vision to share. This is usually a clear sense received when I look at the person concerned - it is as if there is a heavenly presence surrounding them. Around 80% of the time, once this is mentioned to the person in question, there is confirmation from him or her that revelation has been received but also uncertainty as to whether to say anything. This awareness that someone has 'something to share' usually occurs when confirmation is needed that what is sensed is actually from God. I usually *ask* the person in question if they have something to share, rather than telling them that they do! This allows them to have the final say and also allows for the possibility that I may be wrong.

# 11

# Developing a Protocol for Prophecy

> Let two or three prophets speak and let the others weigh what is said.
> 1 CORINTHIANS 14:29

From my experience over the last 45 years in Charismatic churches, this particular piece of advice from Paul is commonly ignored! The verse indicates that prophecy played an important part in the early church and that it was operative to such an extent that there was even need to moderate its use. But before we look more closely at the protocol that Paul advocated for weighing prophecy, we need first to address some questions that this verse poses:

- The first is *who were the prophets* mentioned in 1 Corinthians 14? Was this a specialist group within the congregation who prophesied regularly or was Paul simply referring to those who prophesied on a particular day in a church gathering?

- The next question is *what does it mean to weigh prophecy*?

- The final question is *who were 'the others' who should weigh prophecies*? Did Paul mean the other prophets (narrowly defined) or does 'the others' indicate that everyone present in the gathering could be involved in weighing prophecies?

How we answer these questions will shape the protocol we adopt for weighing prophecy today. Each of these questions is now tackled in turn.

## Is Every Christian a Prophet?

We have already considered the fact that words, including the words prophecy and prophet, have a range of meanings. Context is everything and the precise meaning of a term is determined by its use in a particular sentence, paragraph, or book. This principle helps answer our first question, whether Paul was referring to a narrow group of prophetic ministers in 1 Corinthians 14 or whether he was using the term less precisely. We might broaden this question to ask whether every Christian could be described as a prophet.

The gifts of the Holy Spirit, such as prophecy, are listed in several New Testament passages. Prominent Christian teachers differ as to whether spiritual gifts are all available to everyone in the Church or whether they are distributed more selectively. There are several alternative views:

- We have seen that John Wimber, one of the founders of the Vineyard movement, taught that spiritual gifts were mainly *situational* – in other words, any one of us can receive each and every gift if the situation demands. In this view, God may use any of us to bring healing or working of miracles and we can each prophesy or speak in tongues if that is what is required. We would then all be, potentially at least, prophets.

- On the other hand, some teach that gifts are given to particular people to use regularly rather than being widely distributed to everyone (gifts are described as being *constitutional*). In this view, gifts are resident rather than occasional endowments and people become specialists, with one person regularly prophesying and another, for example, exhibiting gifts of healing. It is possible then that Paul used the term 'prophets' in 1 Corinthians 14 to refer to those who exercised a specialised prophetic role within the Christian community. This view accords with 1 Corinthians 12:27-31 where Paul asks the rhetorical questions, 'Are all apostles? Are all prophets?' and so on.

- A middle view, taking into account the overall evidence found in the New Testament, suggests that, while everyone can potentially prophesy and could be regarded as being a prophet in this sense (Wimber's 'all can play'), few are called to actual prophetic ministry. This view differentiates between the gift, available to all, and the ministry, given to a limited number of people.

Where does this leave Paul's use of the term in 1 Corinthians 14, taking the context into account? The idea that God wants us all to experience the gift of prophecy is implicit in Paul's urging his readers to, 'Earnestly desire the spiritual gifts, especially that you may prophesy' (1 Corinthians 14:1). *This suggests that Paul is using the term 'prophet' in this chapter to refer to anyone who prophesies in a particular gathering.* Elsewhere Paul uses the term to indicate a more specialised role which is differentiated from other ministries in the Church (1 Corinthians 12:28; Ephesians 2:20 & 4:11).

## What Does it Mean to Weigh Prophecy?

Paul talks about 'weighing' what two or three prophets say. The use of the word 'weigh' encourages us to think in terms of how *weighty* or important a particular prophetic word might be. Paul suggested that we find ways to discuss the implications of a prophecy and how much weight to put upon it. By using the word 'weigh', he implies a measuring, almost scrutinising process and that we should never simply assume that a prophetic word is 100% accurate.

It is important to weigh prophecy because no one person, however gifted, has a monopoly on determining what God might be saying to a church. This is a particular danger where the authority of gifted apostolic or prophetic figures is overemphasised and one person, or small group, is assumed to have special access to God's will.[27] Assessing the accuracy and relevance of a prophecy is best done in dialogue with 'the others' and is never the prerogative of just one person.

---

[27] In these circumstances, people are urged either to blindly follow the guidance of their leaders (without weighing it) or, alternatively, to leave the church. This is a form of manipulation.

Before looking at how Paul's injunction to weigh prophecy can be put into practice today, we should consider his context. The churches in the early Christian period met in homes and there was at least one home church in Corinth, possibly more. Their gatherings were informal enough to allow the active participation of many of those present and the intimacy of this setting made it easier to discuss any prophecies than is the case in a large gathering.

Discussion is a valuable practice as, without it, we are prone either to hear and forget prophecies or to store them away without qualification or the input of others. The practice of discussing prophecies to determine their weight is easier in smaller and less formal church gatherings. But whatever our context today, there should always be the understanding, implied or explicitly stated, that we invite others to weigh any prophecies given.

Weighing prophecy is good for both the church and the person who is prophesying. Prophecy can be a cause for pride, which, for the first 1,000 years of the Church, was seen as *the* cardinal sin. Pride is dangerous to our souls and whenever we submit revelation to the wider body of Christ we must seek to do so humbly. Humility is the antidote to pride.

## Who Should Weigh Prophecy?

An interesting question is whether 'the others' who weigh the prophecies are *those with a specialised prophetic ministry* or whether Paul was suggesting that *all those present* in the room should be involved.[28]

He may well have had the whole gathering in view, as some who were not regarded as being prophets would have possessed gifts of discernment, which are vital in such circumstances. In addition, the Spirit is present in the whole body of believers who can, therefore,

---

[28] Paul uses the Greek term 'allos' in this verse, which can indicate another of the same kind. The other available term, 'heteros', can be used to indicate that a different group is in view. The use of allos could, therefore, imply that Paul had other prophets in mind, but this explanation is too simplistic as these terms are often used interchangeably. Paul favours the use of allos elsewhere, so this may simply represent a matter of style rather than having any grammatical significance.

corporately discern the voice of Jesus. We see this dynamic in operation in the Acts of the Apostles. The twelve asked the 'full number of the disciples' to choose seven men to distribute food to the poor and they abided by the decision of the body of believers (Acts 6:1-6). At other times, a group smaller than the full body of believers was involved as in the example of Paul and Barnabas being sent on their first missionary journey. But again, this followed an act of corporate discernment this time involving several leaders in Antioch, rather than everyone in the church (Acts 13:1-4).

In smaller contexts today, such as home groups or small churches, weighing prophecy does not need to be a heavy or even a formal task. It can be done with a light touch when, for example, someone indicates that what is shared with them *does* seem to be relevant to their situation. If there is less certainty the person concerned may indicate that they will think about (weigh) what has been said without immediately affirming its validity. Giving it time is often wise, as a prophecy of major importance will often be confirmed, either circumstantially or through further prophecies being given. If a prophecy is given publicly this affords some safety as it creates scope for feedback or further prophetic input from others present, which may confirm what has already been shared.

We also need to consider how this relates to larger church gatherings since discussion is less easy to facilitate in churches larger than those normally found in New Testament times. However, this may still be possible and a solution that is sometimes employed is that prophetic words are checked with the leader of the meeting before being given publicly. This provides scope for a *certain* degree of discernment although it falls short of what Paul was suggesting in 1 Corinthians 14. Group discernment is not just about assessing the accuracy and weight of a prophecy, it is also an important means of fostering ownership of the future. We are all much more likely to commit to a future that we ourselves have had some part in discerning.

Today, Christian celebrity culture, as well as certain power-laden leadership styles, can imply that the Spirit rests mainly on 'the anointed few' to whom we attribute the ability for discernment. Simply accepting a prophecy without exercising discernment is an abdication of personal responsibility and makes for bad 'followership'.

Having the chance to give our opinion is important, even if ultimately an outcome at variance with our own thoughts and feelings, but supported by the majority, is followed. If we abandon our critical faculties, we may lay ourselves open to being manipulated or even become vulnerable to abusive control. Whether it was the whole gathered church or a smaller group that Paul had in mind, prophecies are to be weighed. The mechanics of weighing prophecy will be outlined in the next chapter after having explored how we actually administrate prophecy in our gatherings.

## Spontaneity & Order

> When you come together, each one has a hymn, a lesson, a revelation, a tongue or an interpretation. Let all things be done for building up.
> 1 CORINTHIANS 14:26

In this verse, Paul addressed the issue of how the Corinthian church could organise various possible contributions to be shared in a church gathering. The first thing to notice is that many people took part, as is indicated by the phrase 'each one'. Church was participatory, with 'each one' playing a part and it may have been the case that there were, in fact, too many contributions in Corinth. If so, a way to be selective needed to be found to ensure that people actually benefitted from the contributions given, rather than being overloaded. One principle which Paul highlighted was to consider whether what was shared would build others up in their faith.

It is unclear whether the different contributions that Paul lists were pre-planned or more spontaneous. More 'charismatic' readers will favour the spontaneous option and more classical evangelicals will favour the idea that contributions were planned beforehand! It is likely that there was a combination of both.

The balance between spontaneous and planned contributions is not always easy to achieve, but *it is unwise to act as though immediately inspired prophecy must always be given the higher priority.* There are several reasons why this is undesirable:

1. Firstly, **when we gather together, we need to bear in mind that this is primarily for worship**. We meet to give thanks to God for all that he has done, particularly for the redemption he achieved on our behalf. Worship acts as a reminder of this and it focuses us on God's great acts of deliverance. We need this to prevent amnesia from setting in because the pressure of life (or the distraction of pleasure) easily fills our vision. In this respect, Christian worship resembles aspects of Judaism, such as honouring the sabbath and annual religious festivals, that were designed to keep alive the story of God's intervention in history. Worship includes everything we do when we meet - prayer, reading scripture and hearing a talk or sermon. As Paul reminds us, 'when we gather for worship, each has a psalm, a teaching, a revelation, a tongue, an interpretation' for our edification and for the common good (1 Corinthians 14:26). Components interact with and enhance each other, so that concepts explained in a talk can inspire us to worship God in a more enlightened or more wholehearted way or might prompt us to read a psalm of exultation to God and so on. The popular idea that worship equates only to singing God's praises, essential though that is, is far too narrow a view. As well as keeping the big story front and centre, we also need to make room for prophecy, perhaps to (occasionally) communicate new vision for the church and sometimes to have 'notices', but we must never lose sight of the fact that we gather primarily to celebrate what Christ has achieved through his Cross and resurrection.[29] Gathering together is an opportunity to *look back* to the victory of God and to *look forward* to the coming of the kingdom in all its fullness. Our gatherings are meant to consist of a varied diet, as Paul outlined in 1 Corinthians 12-14, including hearing God's word to us in the Bible and through prophecy - but if there are too many prophecies, we ourselves rather than God can unwittingly become the focus of worship.

---

[29] Worship is quashed when church leaders *mainly* see church gatherings as an opportunity to communicate their vision or to announce what the church is doing. 'Notices' can also distract from worship.

2. Another reason to limit prophetic contributions is that **when God is saying something he often speaks to and through a number of different people.** Revelation is received by each one in differing ways and covers slightly different aspects of the theme in question. The reception of prophecy may happen for some during the course of a gathering but for others, a prophecy may have been received beforehand, possibly even incubating over a long period of time. As one person shares publicly what he or she has received, often it sparks and encourages the contribution of others. There is, however, little need for the theme to be expressed or reiterated multiple times and Paul limits the number of prophetic contributions in any one church gathering to two or three. It can be overwhelming if there are more than three prophetic words with many people sharing what they sense God is saying. If too many different things are communicated then the main prophetic thrust can easily be lost.

3. The third reason for limiting prophetic input is that **the long slow preparation involved in crafting a talk or sermon needs to be honoured.** Adequate time needs to be allowed to ensure that teaching gifts have their rightful place in a church gathering. If someone spends hours seeking God for the content of a talk, then what they have to say is likely to be important and timely for the church to hear. It may also be prophetic. If we give more space to those who receive immediate revelation, we are in danger of wrongly elevating prophecy and devaluing other contributions.

In summary, Paul portrays prophecy as operating within a highly interactive context which includes space being given for others' comments on what had been shared. Paul's advice to limit contributions is often ignored in many charismatic circles with frustrating and exhausting results. When one person after another gets up to say something, 'quality control' is lacking and, because too much is said, much of what is shared is lost. Allowing this scenario may ensure that everyone has a chance to contribute, but, although laudable in its motivation, it produces chaotic results. An overly permissive attitude also avoids the need to gently confront those who overvalue their contribution and have too much to say too often. Adhering to the protocol that Paul suggested in 1 Corinthians 14 helps us identify more precisely those things that God is seeking to communicate through prophecy. His comment on tongues could also be applied to situations where good governance of prophecy is lacking: 'If the bugle gives an indistinct sound, who will get ready for battle?' (1 Corinthians 14:8).

## 12

# Weighing Prophecy

We have explored the protocol which Paul outlined for delivering and weighing prophecy and at this point we delve more deeply into the mechanics of discernment, drawing together several of the themes touched on earlier. Because receiving revelation is subjective, human elements come into play in prophecy and we need to discern the activity of the Holy Spirit and differentiate this from our feelings, thoughts, and wishes. In addition, we must be alert to the activity of more malign spiritual influences that may affect our moods and feelings. But the first test to apply is more objective as we determine whether a particular prophecy conforms to the witness of scripture.

## Prophecy & Orthodoxy

Genuine prophecies will not contradict the revelation recorded in the Bible. Paul emphasised the importance of doctrinal correctness in evaluating revelation when he wrote that nobody who is inspired by the Spirit will say 'Jesus is cursed' (1 Corinthians 12:3). Commentators are uncertain about the context in which someone would make such a claim but presumably this was a teaching dominant in certain quarters. Jesus is now exalted above every other name (Philippians 2:9) and Paul regarded any prophetic statement to the contrary as being false. Prophecy today will not deviate from the teaching of scripture, neither will it add to our knowledge of God, although it may reinforce and bring home certain truths, such as seen in the Spirit-inspired declaration, 'Jesus is Lord!' (1 Corinthians 12:3).

A similar point is made in John's letters. Certain teachers were promoting the idea that Jesus was an angelic spiritual being who only *appeared* to be flesh and blood. This teaching, known as Docetism, implied that he was not fully human - a serious error promoted by those regarded as being false prophets. Doctrinal correctness is highly important, especially in areas such as the nature of Jesus, and John countered Docetism when he wrote that 'every spirit that confesses that Jesus Christ has come in the flesh is from God' (1 John 4:2).

Clearly, Christians do not see eye to eye on every aspect of doctrine, but the basics (such as the Trinity, the Cross, and the need for faith in Jesus) are unalterable. Paul warns his readers not to be impressed by the outward appearance of the messenger but to look to the soundness of what is being communicated (Galatians 1:8). We could rephrase this today, 'Stick with the message of the gospel, even if an impressive prophet with amazing gifts should tell you of their new revelation'.

## Beware False Prophets!

> But false prophets also arose among the people, just as there will be false teachers among you, who will secretly bring in destructive heresies, even denying the Master who bought them, bringing upon themselves swift destruction.
> 2 PETER 2:1

The topic of weighing prophecy often brings to mind those passages, particularly in the Old Testament, which refer to false prophets. Peter's words (quoted above) identify a false prophet as *someone who leads others away from following God* into idolatry. This is particularly the case in Deuteronomy where the death penalty was commanded for those who prophesied in the name of other gods, and we should remember that the worship of these other gods sometimes involved child sacrifice or engaging in cult prostitution.

In other instances, false prophets are spoken against, but the death penalty is not enacted:

> My hand will be against the prophets who see false visions and who give lying divinations. They shall not be in the council of my people, nor be enrolled in the register of the house of Israel, nor

shall they enter the land of Israel.
EZEKIEL 13:9

Although not put to death, they were excluded from God's blessing and were barred from living in the Promised Land. This was not an inconsequential matter and there were serious repercussions for those involved. Similarly, when 400 royal prophets prophesied falsely, the king of Israel did *not* have them killed, presumably because they were not advocating the worship of other gods (1 Kings 22:6).

When we come to the New Testament, there are similar warnings to be on the lookout for false prophets, who are characterised by a desire to exploit others for their own ends. *They are identified by the general tenor of their lives and the results of their ministry* - particularly if they lead people astray rather than build them up in their faith (Matthew 7:15). As previously mentioned, this particular 'test' requires that prophets are known and seen by others, rather than be distant remote figures who are mainly hidden from the public view.

When we evaluate prophecy today, we are dealing mostly with issues of tone and accuracy rather than with the issue of false prophets. We may also wrongly presume that our opinions and God's coincide. Nathan, who is regarded as an exemplary prophet, mistakenly encouraged David to build a temple. Subsequently, he was corrected by God, but no punishment was required as this represented a genuine mistake rather than a deliberate attempt to mislead David (2 Samuel 7:1-7).

There is a definite need to confront false prophets, but when it is more a question of poor practice a different approach is called for. A supportive environment is conducive to honing prophetic skills - a church culture where mistakes are not only made and acknowledged, recognising that we are all fallible, but also where those who prophesy are encouraged to persist and improve their prophetic practice (as previously outlined in the section on a learning culture). The very fact that we are encouraged to weigh a prophetic word implies that *despite the best will in the world we will get it wrong at times,* but this does not mean we are false prophets. The factors in play include a lack of experience with prophetic gifts or confusing our own wishes with the prompting of the Holy Spirit. In addition, we 'prophesy in part' and even when God has given revelation to someone, that person is unlikely to perceive every aspect of a situation (1 Corinthians 13:9).

## Exercising Discernment

Alongside the objective test of conformity to scripture, there are other ways in which to evaluate prophecy which come under the heading of discernment. Discernment answers questions such as: 'Is this prophecy from God or from another source?'; 'Are there elements that we might affirm but others about which we are less certain?'; and 'Is any action required arising from the content of this prophetic word?'

Perhaps the most common challenge is to decide what proportion of a prophecy is of God and whether someone is adding their own interpretation to what has been revealed. Again, we need to bear in mind that God's revelation will be fully accurate, but our delivery may be less so. It is easy to jump to conclusions when God reveals something to us. We may, for example, have a strong impression that God is about to bless someone, and at the same time be aware that they have financial needs. We can easily but mistakenly put two and two together and presume that finances will soon be released when, in reality, God intends to bless them in other areas.

Many years ago, someone known to me received a vision whilst praying for a lady who was going through an extraordinarily difficult time. The vision was simply of the person concerned in a prison cell. The person who received the vision wrongly assumed that she needed psychological release in some way and prayed accordingly. A short time later, however, it came to light that she faced an actual short-term prison sentence which might have explained how flustered she became during the prayer.

We see a biblical example of presumption when Agabus prophesied to Paul concerning the likelihood of his being taken captive if he went ahead with his plan to visit Jerusalem. Agabus wrongly assumed that this meant that Paul should not go there. We can easily interpret what we sense from God in ways which reflect our own hopes and aspirations for the person concerned. The lesson for prophecy today is to realise that *our assumptions and wishes will influence how we interpret a prophecy and, therefore, the words we choose to deliver it.*

Prophecy is usually received as a strong inner conviction, and we then seek to convey in words what is sensed inwardly. Our personality will come into play in this process. If we have a strong drive to avoid difficulties, we tend to stress the encouraging aspects of a prophecy and downplay elements that suggest that hard times may lie ahead.

This calls for self-awareness combined with the practice of discernment. Determining the mix of human and divine elements in a particular prophetic word is a major component in determining how much weight to put upon it.

Discernment in any area of life is a skill honed through practice and we can grow in our ability to sift the chaff from the wheat. I have spent many hours looking for signs of fish in lakes and rivers and I can often detect their presence by observing almost imperceptible changes in the pattern of ripples on the surface of the water. This comes through experience, wasting a lot of time to develop a 'sixth sense' that is difficult to describe to other people. This is actually the ability to piece together very small visual clues, but we may not consciously register those clues, so it feels more like a sense. We gradually develop a feel for something and this is similar to growing in the discernment of prophetic gifts.

To change the analogy, growing in our ability to discern the voice of God is like listening to a piece of music and being able to pick out individual instruments. Perhaps we learn to detect the presence of an oboe or bassoon, or we might hear the difference in tonal quality between a Telecaster and a Stratocaster guitar. The discernment of prophecy, including the ability to distinguish it from other forms of subjective experience, is just as subtle a process and it grows with practice. No process for determining the mix of human and divine elements in a prophecy is 100% accurate, but there are several helpful guidelines. These include:

## The 'feel' of the prophecy

Jesus stated that his words were life and an important factor is whether or not a prophecy communicates something of the life of God to the recipient. Jesus talked about the outflow of the Spirit in our lives using the analogy of a river of living, bubbling, refreshing water (John 7:37-39). It is likely, therefore, that the majority of prophecies today will have this life-giving, refreshing quality about them. Although God may speak a word of judgement through someone, this is uncommon and it requires considerable discernment before it is accepted as such. Anything that could be construed as being corrective in any way needs to be filtered through God's grace and compassion.

### Does it resonate with the recipient?

An important element in discernment is whether the recipient of the prophecy can relate to what is being said. Does it ring true? A prophetic word is not an objective statement and it should not be received purely based on our respect for the person prophesying (although that respect is an important factor in our weighing any prophecy given). The voice of Jesus will be recognised as such by the recipient, in keeping with his statement that his sheep know his voice (John 10:27-30). The content of a prophecy and its tone of delivery need to resonate with the hearer.

### The gift of discerning of spirits

It is interesting to note that in the list of gifts in 1 Corinthians 12 certain gifts are paired, tongues and the interpretation of tongues being an obvious example. What may be less obvious is that prophecy and discerning of spirits are also juxtaposed and this may indicate that these two gifts complement one another. Discerning of spirits provides clarity concerning the source of a particular prophetic word but we need to distinguish the gift of discernment from another gift that some people have – the gift of suspicion!

Discerning of spirits allows us to sense whether a prophecy originates with the Holy Spirit or expresses our own hopes and fears. We can be misled by demonic spirits or be subject to either adverse moods or over-optimism. If we are undiscerning, we will accept everything as genuine and eventually we will become disillusioned when prophecies prove to have been wrong.

### Consensus provides a safeguard

There is no scientific or wholly objective process for judging a particular prophecy. Apart from conformity to scripture, we rely on subjective elements, including the existence of consensus about the likely authenticity of a particular word.

An interesting parallel is the process by which some books were included in the Bible and others were not. One element among others was identifying those books that were commonly regarded as containing the true word of God. This was clearly subjective and it relied on developing a consensus. Although there was agreement concerning most books the Catholic, Orthodox and Protestant canons have some important differences. This demonstrates that coming to a consensus is not an infallible process and we need humility when it comes to the evaluation of prophecy, even when we have reached agreement.

## Discerning who the prophecy applies to

Another point to note is that something of what individuals sense God is saying may actually relate more to themselves than to the church as a whole or to other individuals. This is particularly the case where there is 'a flow' of prophecy in a gathering and many people receive revelation. Often the revelation received simply confirms that what others are giving voice to is applicable to one's own life. It is a skill to differentiate between what God is saying to us personally and what God wants to say to the whole congregation.

## Major prophecies will usually be confirmed

> *The Holy Spirit testifies in every city* that imprisonment and afflictions await me.
> ACTS 20:23

Paul received the same prophetic message repeatedly *in every city*. We too should expect confirmation of any major prophecies received from others. I recently heard an example of someone who was 'given a scripture' by a friend who believed that it applied to her situation. Within the space of a few weeks two other people mentioned the same verses to her. This would suggest that God had indeed highlighted the scripture although other tests of genuineness might still need to be considered.

A prophetic word will usually be in keeping with the journey God has taken someone on thus far. It may simply confirm that the path along which God is already directing the person is the right one but whenever God is seeking to radically redirect us it is likely that this will be confirmed in a number of different ways.

## Recognise off-limits topics for prophecy

There are certain topics which, in my opinion, should be off-limits for prophecy. We need to be extremely wary if, for example, someone prophesies that we might marry a particular person. God can and does guide us in such matters, as evidenced in a number of Old Testament stories, but we would expect there to be mutual attraction and other confirmatory aspects to the relationship. As the saying goes 'if you get married on a prophecy, you'll need a prophecy every day to stay married!'

## Prophecy as the Exercise of Power

In addition, an awareness of any possible power dynamics helps us discern whether or not to accept a prophetic word. There exists the potential for misuse of power through prophecy. At an extreme end of the spectrum are those who use prophecy as a cover to control others or bolster their reputation. Prophecy can be attractive to those with narcissistic personality traits as it provides a way to exercise ministry that might impress others.

Narcissism is a concept based on the myth of Narcissus, who fell in love with his own reflection in a pool of water. Narcissistic leaders outwardly have marked self-confidence and this projects a strongly competent image that can be attractive to others. They may be charming but may actually lack genuine empathy and see others as a means to achieving their own ends. Even though they might not have a full-blown narcissistic personality disorder, people who strongly exhibit these traits often bolster their self-image at the expense of others.

Many people have mild narcissistic traits and some Christian leaders, as well as those in other religious settings, exhibit tendencies towards narcissism. We all have dysfunctional aspects to our personalities, so this is not intended to be judgemental but simply to acknowledge that caution is wise when leaders, however impressive in operating prophetic gifts, exhibit marked narcissistic traits.

## Learning from Traditional Discernment Processes

We can learn much from those who, in past ages, have explored the topic of discernment. One such person was Ignatius of Loyola, the founder of the Jesuit order. He kept a record of his experiences of God, and this became a classic text for Christian spirituality, *The Spiritual Exercises*. Part of Ignatius's quest was to be able to distinguish between the source of various inner impulses which he experienced and he referred to this process as 'discerning of spirits'. He saw this as the ability to distinguish between thoughts and feelings which were inspired by God and those which were of demonic origin.

In order to discern the source of these impulses he developed his own terminology using the terms consolation and desolation. By '**consolation**' Ignatius was describing the experience of moving closer to God, in which case we become aware that faith or love is growing within us. Consolation is not to be confused with 'feeling happy', since a course of action which we believe God wants us to take might actually be challenging and initially cause some anxiety; God's will might also bring us into conflict with others, but despite these personal challenges we nonetheless feel we are being drawn closer to God.

**Desolation** is experienced when we are far from God's presence and we feel fear or have profound doubts. We become preoccupied with ourselves rather than with God or other people and desolation drives us towards isolation whereas consolation connects us to others. When we experience desolation, we may seek false consolation in destructive behaviours such as overindulging in food or alcohol. These activities lead to a further downward spiral, whereas consolation creates hope and renews our vision.

My description of Ignatian discernment is an oversimplification of a process which is learned gradually and refined through experience. It is also notable that it is most often exercised within a community rather than something done alone. Ignatius was interested in guidance rather than in prophecy, but he highlighted several key elements that are relevant both to someone giving a prophecy and to its recipient.

If we believe we have received a prophecy *for* someone, Ignatian principles help us discern whether it brings a sense of consolation, a positive sense of hope and a future. It will lead us to desolation, with accompanying hopelessness and fear, if it is not from God.

When we receive a prophecy *from* another person, we can also apply the test of consolation or desolation. It is not that we ask ourselves does the prophecy make us happy or sad, but whether or not it draws us closer to God and deeper into his will. I would recommend a study of Ignatian discernment for those of us who regularly prophesy or need to weigh prophecy.

The next chapter broadens the discussion of discernment by evaluating certain experiences that are often taken to be forms of prophetic revelation.

# 13

# Prophecy, Intuitions & Hunches

I have had a number of different experiences which have made me think more deeply about the practice of prophecy in the Church. In particular, there are instances where unchurched people also appear to have received revelation, the nature of which is seemingly not unlike that received in churches (and at conferences) where people are prayed for or prophesied over. Although this observation has not resulted in doubting that Christian prophecy is genuinely inspired by the Spirit, it has raised questions for me as to whether other processes may sometimes be operative. This chapter is, therefore, somewhat speculative, but addresses important issues that relate both to the discernment of prophecy and the credibility of the Charismatic Church.

## A Rather Fishy Tale

Some years ago, whilst on holiday on a remote Scottish island, I was flyfishing for trout in a small river. I was fairly successful, having wasted many an hour in similar circumstances. I met another fisherman on the riverbank, whom I later learned was a prominent sculptor taking a break with other artist friends. Unlike me, he was not using a homemade fly rod – he had one of the best that money could buy. Unlike me, and despite his superior kit, he had never caught a trout before and he was asking my advice. I shared with him the wisdom I had accrued through my misspent adulthood pursuing fish and very soon he had a trout on the bank. He was extremely pleased and invited me for a celebratory dram of single malt whisky. Over a drink in his cottage, he said to me, 'You are either a doctor or a vicar'. Actually, I was both (although I would use the term church leader rather than vicar). How did he know? I guess my demeanour gave it away and that he was an astute observer with experience of both doctors and vicars.

Arthur Conan Doyle based his character Sherlock Holmes on an Edinburgh physician who could, through minute observations, often tell the occupation of his patients or reveal other details concerning their lives. Sherlock was similarly gifted in assessing those who came to him for help in crime detection. Stage magicians sometimes use similar techniques, as do many charlatan clairvoyants. These are examples not of revelation from God but of the ability to 'read people' and as such raise the possibility that a similar ability could lie behind *some* examples of what in Christian circles are assumed to be words of knowledge.

## Our Ability to Detect Subliminal Clues

Sherlock Holmes and my fisherman friend both engaged in a very conscious process to assess people but there can also be a more subliminal process that happens outside our conscious awareness. We all have wide experience with different types of people and we learn to rapidly detect clues about the person in front of us even if we have never met them before. It is said that when meeting someone for the first time, we automatically assimilate hundreds of pieces of information about them. This subconscious process may involve details about their age, ethnicity, culture and background, how they dress, health and physique, height and weight, attractiveness, and even details about their personality and confidence. Our past experience often helps us to correctly predict certain characteristics about a new acquaintance, without always fully registering the exact nature of these clues. This is not revelation although it may feel as if it is because we cannot necessarily pinpoint why we seem to know particular things about a stranger.

30 years ago I started a Master of Arts in Counselling degree. On our first day of the course, we were divided into pairs. This was before we had had a chance to get acquainted with one another and so

effectively were strangers. We then took part in a series of exercises, one of which involved saying to the person we were paired with: 'I imagine that you...' Relying on conjecture and our perception, we proceeded to give voice to what we felt might be true of the other person. It was a playful exercise, done with a light touch, but I remember being extremely surprised at the accuracy of my partner's perceptions of me and mine of her. This included whether we had children, the style of car we drove and other seemingly random details. Of course, our guesses were not always accurate but many of these imaginative leaps were quite insightful.

This experience reminded me of several occasions where I had witnessed Christians ministering to one another. I believe that in many of these cases, genuine revelation imparted by the Holy Spirit was received. But in other instances, I suspect that people were actually picking up subliminal clues about the person for whom they were praying. Some of our reasonably accurate perceptions may it seems have a more natural explanation – not all have come as revelation, as a gift of the Holy Spirit. I am reminded of an occasion some years ago when an elderly pub landlady remarkably accurately summed up the personality of a friend with whom I was sitting and whom she had never met before. She, of course, was accustomed to meeting many people who until they entered her pub, were otherwise complete strangers. Naturally acquired (subliminal) knowledge is, of course, completely legitimate and potentially very valuable. It helps us navigate relationships and predict when we should be trusting or wary of someone. That said, however, we do need to be cautious and try to discern the origin of our knowledge about others because people may place great significance on what is said if revelation from God is believed to be involved. Imagine, for instance, if my fishing companion had been a Christian and had told me that he sensed I was a doctor. He might have felt this sense was confirmation from God concerning my vocation and have encouraged me, for example, to persist with medicine.

## Other Sources of Revelation

The suggestion that we consider alternative explanations before deciding that someone *has* had a revelation from God might seem perverse. It is, however, important to be discerning because of the weight put on genuine revelation. God's work stands up to examination.[30]

As well as recognising our ability to pick up clues subliminally, a clear distinction must also be made between genuine knowledge from God and that received from 'familiar spirits'. But further possibilities should also be considered. What follows is an attempt to make sense of several commonly encountered phenomena and is offered tentatively for further thought and debate.

For instance, many people, both in and outside the Church, report premonitions concerning the future. It is also a common experience that someone comes to mind just before that person gets in contact with us or we unexpectedly 'bump into' them. At times, we might become very aware of a close friend or relative only to find that they are in danger or are unwell. Coincidences such as these are sometimes referred to as 'synchronicity', a term coined by Carl Jung. There were several such stories in my own family of origin, despite their having no clear faith commitment.

How we explain these phenomena will depend on several factors, such as our personal experience, our degree of scepticism and our theology. These sorts of occurrences have prompted me to take a variety of possibilities into account in considering the origin of our knowledge concerning others. I am aware that these issues are rarely explored but we need to engage with them to have a thought-through approach to revelation which enables us to be discerning and to give a credible account of what we believe. Some possible explanations will now be explored.

## The Potential to Sense Information 'Spiritually'

For a decade I trained and then worked in a psychotherapy unit based in the grounds of a regional psychiatric hospital. I was attracted to work in this unit which employed the so-called psychodynamic approach. This involved more than simply understanding clients in

---

[30] I admire the fact that no apparent healing at Lourdes is accepted as being genuine without a thorough medical investigation to ensure that there is no other reasonable explanation.

terms of human psychology. There was, of course, psychological understanding employed but psychodynamic therapy involves becoming aware of what happens within us as therapists when with the client. We learned to notice what was being evoked as we spent time with a particular person – known technically as countertransference. So, for example, if as the therapist, we experience feelings of boredom whilst being with the client then those feelings could themselves be clues as to the actual experience of the client in a particular scenario which she was describing.

As part of my initial training, I would see my supervisor each week and read through a report I had prepared outlining one chosen session with a client that week. My supervisor was very skilled and experienced and on several occasions, he made comments which seemed unrelated to my presentation of the client's story. These comments were based not on any logical analysis but on his own more subjective internal processes. Initially, I found the disconnection between what I had presented and his reflections quite disconcerting. What surprised me was that the client would often raise the very same issues my supervisor had mentioned in the next session. This was, I believe, an example of intuition, based on an awareness of an internal process. Because of professional experience, skill and expertise, my supervisor had become highly trained to take note of feelings evoked within himself as he listened to my presentation of the client in question.

How do we explain such experiences? It may be that as created beings animated by the breath of God, we have an innate ability to sense things in our spirit. If this natural explanation is the case, this is not limited to Christian believers and is not as such direct revelation from God. Rather it is an ability to sense things about others on a spiritual, not just a physical or intellectual, level. After all, whether or not someone has faith, as Christians we believe that as humans we are all spiritual beings. I am *not* suggesting that we are all connected by some form of spiritual world wide web as found in certain New Age teachings since what is described appears to operate on an individual-to-individual level. This does not, however, mean that all such knowledge is helpful as it can be used for ill as well as for good.

Another example of how we might sense something in our spirit is when we experience particular places as being either good or threatening. Again this is a common experience and not limited to people of faith. My wife recently was in conversation with a humanist friend, who described parts of a particular town as being 'really horrible', saying that she hated its feel and atmosphere.

I am a trustee at a retreat centre in Wales called Ffald y Brenin, which is Welsh for *The Sheepfold of the King*. There have been several occasions when tradespeople and couriers have visited the site and had a profound sense of peace. A recent example involved someone making a delivery to the centre. He had no idea that it was a retreat centre, but as he drove up the long steep drive he was uncharacteristically tearful. He asked the staff what exactly went on at the centre because he could not understand why he felt so moved as he approached it. This sort of experience is common at sites that the ancient Celtic Christians described as 'thin places'.

These experiences, involving our knowledge of people and places, need to be considered when we apply ourselves to discern what is or is not revelation from God. How we interpret these phenomena is determined by our views of what it means to be human. The suggestion here is that we all have an inner spiritual life, whether or not we realise it, and even if we do not have a Christian faith. It is commonly accepted by theologians that we retain certain aspects of the image of God despite our sin. This residual image is usually thought to be the basis for conscience and of a sense of moral responsibility. What is suggested here is that our spirit may play an even more active role, one that includes the potential to sense things spiritually.

## Non-Believers & Revelation

The possibility that, as part of our humanity, we all have an innate spiritual sense is important for us to consider. It is evident that God sometimes speaks directly to those who are not yet Christians. If this were not the case, then no one would move from unbelief to faith. The question is more whether God speaks to those with no Christian faith about matters other than salvation and the biblical record suggests that this can and does happen.

Abimelech, a pagan king in the ancient Near East, is one example (Genesis 20:3). Abraham was worried that if he admitted that Sarah was his wife he would be killed – she was very attractive and the king might want to take her. In fact, the king did desire her but he was warned by God in a dream not to approach her because she was Abraham's wife. We see a further example in Genesis 31:24. God came to Laban, Jacob's father-in-law, in a dream, warning him not to speak to Jacob, who was fleeing with his daughters and possessions! God revealed this to Laban even though he was not part of the family of faith.

Even more curious is the somewhat bizarre story of Balaam's donkey in Numbers 22. In this case, an animal had been given the ability to see an angel before its presence was revealed to its owner. God is simply not limited in any way in his ability to communicate with and through his created beings and creatures. These examples suggest that God sometimes communicates directly with those who are not part of the household of faith, in some cases to protect those who are. God also communicated directly with Pilate's wife in a dream, telling her that Jesus was innocent and prompting her to warn Pilate 'not to have anything to do with him' (Matthew 27:19).

## Other Sources of Knowledge

However, malign forces and powers are also at work in our world, breaking into people's lives to cause havoc, chaos and destruction. In Acts 16, we see that demonic spirits are a counterfeit source of knowledge - a slave girl in Philippi was able to exercise a gift of divination. She followed Paul and his companion around the city proclaiming that they were messengers sent by God. This was, of course, true but it was disruptive and created unwelcome attention. The testimony of this slave girl augmented her credibility and falsely bolstered her reputation as a true prophet.

Interestingly, Paul waited several days before dealing with this although from the outset he must have known that her proclamation was the manifestation of a demonic spirit. He ministered complete deliverance and freedom to this girl, no doubt an unwilling slave of both her owner and the spirit. This was, in fact, the reason why Paul and Silas were imprisoned in Philippi, since depriving the girl of her gift also deprived her owner of his source of income.

We know from reading scripture that dreams and visions can be mediated through angelic beings and that knowledge can also be communicated through angels rather than being received directly from God. As in the case of other sources of revelation, discernment as to the source of dreams and visions is critical. Malign spiritual forces, as well as deceitful people, will often masquerade as angels of light, mimicking God's power and abilities in order to deceive us (2 Corinthians 11:4). It is for this reason that discernment of spirits is so important.[31] John Michael Talbot has described an ability to discern the spirits of both people and spiritual forces in an almost visual way. He reports being able to 'see' fallen angels surrounding people but adds that this is not a pleasant experience.[32]

In this chapter we have outlined three broad categories which aid in classifying the source of knowledge concerning the people and situations we encounter:

## Negative Sources
Accurate knowledge can have a demonic origin, as in the case of the Philippian slave girl. This sort of knowledge needs to be clearly identified as harmful and then resisted and rejected.

## Neutral Sources
If suggestions made previously concerning subliminal observation or spiritual sensing are correct, it means that knowledge can also come from more neutral sources. In such cases, knowledge is still valuable but it is not to be relied on or considered to be as important as revelation from God. Knowledge obtained through neutral sources can be used with good or bad effect.

## Positive Sources
This is the revelation that comes directly from the Holy Spirit or is received via an angelic intermediary. It is instructive and informative, giving insight and revelation about people and situations, of which we would otherwise not have awareness. It is instrumental in God's purposes being outworked.

---

[31] We should note that, in scripture, neither angels nor demonic forces conform to stereotypes. Angels that appear to people in the Old Testament are often mistaken for ordinary humans (and can, therefore, be entertained unawares).
[32] J M Talbot, *Exploring the Gifts of the Spirit.*

In summary, most within the Charismatic Movement accept that divine revelation is the basis for a number of the gifts of the Spirit and that revelation is given, usually though not exclusively, to God's people, to enable them to further God's will on earth in their own context. Alongside this appreciation is the generally accepted concept that demonic spirits or angels can also be a source of knowledge since this has a sound biblical basis.

The situation, however, may be more complex than described. It may be that as well as the possibility of receiving knowledge and insight from God the Holy Spirit, or even through an angelic messenger or a demonic source, we need to consider more natural ways of acquiring knowledge about people or situations as possible sources of 'revelation'. This includes our subliminal observations of others as well as the idea that, as human beings made in God's image, we might also possess a natural ability to sense things spiritually.

# 14

# Growing in Prophecy

The final chapters of this book explore a number of issues that are relevant to the exercise of prophecy in the Charismatic and Pentecostal Movements. Some of the methods used to develop the gift of prophecy are considered as well as how we might reframe prophecy today in order to rescue it from less desirable practices that, over the years, have grown up in some quarters.

## Developing Prophetic Gifts – 3 Approaches

With the realisation that prophecy is such an important component of life in the Spirit, attention is focused on encouraging more widespread use of this gift. In broad terms, three approaches concerning growing in understanding and practice of prophecy are currently in use:

- What tends to be seen in the Bible is a model of **apprenticeship**, an approach which aids the development of gifts and character. This is usually employed where specialised prophetic ministry is the intended outcome. It is effective but because of its time-consuming nature is not used widely, since it requires the creation of ongoing relationships for learning.

- **Learning to prophesy in local** contexts. The main arenas for developing prophetic gifts are local and relational, such as those found in churches, home groups or intentional Christian communities. These contexts can provide suitable conditions conducive to the gifts being exercised and honed over time.

- In addition, over the past 40 years, there has been a proliferation of conferences, **training events and discipleship schools** all designed to enable Christians to prophesy. These resources have helped many to exercise prophetic gifts within the Church and in their everyday lives. Some training courses focus on so-called 'prophetic evangelism' whereby evangelists, often on the street or in shopping malls, engage people in conversation by using God-given knowledge.

We will briefly explore these different approaches, which may, of course, be employed by one and the same person at different times. Some critique, particularly focusing on training events, is then offered.

## Apprenticeship Models of Training

Effectively, Jesus' disciples engaged in an apprenticeship relationship with him, first observing how he ministered to people and then imitating what they had seen modelled by him. They employed the same approach as he did and had feedback to help them refine their skills (Mark 9:29; Luke 10:1-17).

This is similar to the process employed when I was training as a medical student and in my years as a junior doctor. We observed carefully how a more senior doctor performed a particular procedure, perhaps a minor operation, and then under supervision undertook the same procedure ourselves. Once proficient we were let loose on our own and, in time, taught others more junior than ourselves.

This process is more effective than simply acquiring head knowledge, important though that is, and this apprenticeship model can be crucial for our learning and development. Personally, I have had the privilege of working and travelling with two very different church leaders from whom I learned much, primarily through observation. If I am in certain situations I think to myself 'what would John or Dave do?' (I rarely ask 'what would Jesus do?' as he often seemed to do the opposite of what I might predict!)

We see this model used many times in the Bible. Joshua was Moses' understudy, which required much devotion and dedication to his teacher. Elisha's apprenticeship with Elijah entailed great personal sacrifice, leaving home, career and family. He had to 'learn the ropes' but more than this he picked up his teacher's spirit and received Elijah's prophetic anointing at the end of his life, as he ascended to the presence of God. This was not a quick prayer for impartation; it was the culmination of a long process of discipleship which involved living with and following his teacher.

This is similar to a common model used in New Testament times where learning involved a close personal involvement between rabbi and disciple. The disciple followed behind the rabbi and was said to have been covered in the dust from the rabbi's feet! We also see in scripture what could be described as prophetic training schools. The 'sons of the prophets' was one such school, existing alongside the close relationship between Elijah and Elisha yet slightly removed. While these disciples received training and learned to exercise prophetic gifts, they sometimes failed to pick up the values Elisha imbibed from his personal, close relationship with Elijah. This was evident in their callous declaration of knowledge revealed to them that Elijah would soon be taken from them (2 Kings 2:5). Nonetheless, following Elijah's departure, Elisha remained with these sons of the prophets, for they were learners too.

## Learning to Prophesy in Local Contexts

The apprenticeship model, as described above, can be taken as the gold standard in facilitating the development of prophetic ministers. But more commonly the aim is to develop prophecy more generally rather than to produce specialists. In addition, the time and personnel involved in providing such intensive training may, in fact, make an apprenticeship model impractical for most contexts. Yet there are valuable lessons to be learned from apprenticeship, particularly the way in which we learn best by observing others, putting it into practice ourselves and then possibly having feedback.

An essential aspect of this process, transferable to less intensive learning contexts, is being given the opportunity to put into practice what we have ourselves observed being done. This allows us both to make mistakes and to adjust things as we go along, as we discover what works well and what works less well. This creative process also allows us to develop our own unique style, depending on our personality and particular mix of prophetic gifting. The best context for this is the local church, especially if there are others more practised in prophetic gifts than we are and if the opportunity is given for prophecy to be weighed. As mentioned in a previous chapter, one Pentecostal church provided this learning environment for me and subsequently my learning developed in other contexts.

Prophetic gifts are refined as we minister in communities of God's people and it is important that we do not pursue prophecy in isolation. That is not to decry the potential value of attending courses to broaden our understanding of prophecy, nor is it to suggest that we cannot learn from books or teaching (in a local church, at conferences, or on the internet). These can be helpful as long as we are aware that *ongoing and in-depth 'everyday' relationships provide the most important context for learning.* Connectedness with respected people in our church communities saves us from becoming deceived or falling prey to unsubstantiated and untested claims, such as conspiracy theories. This is a particular risk if we turn to the offerings of unknown sources on the internet – or if we consider that to be the primary forum for ministry.

## Training Courses, Events & Conferences

While the benefit to individuals and churches has been enormous, strictly speaking, some would consider it wrong to suggest that people can be *trained* to prophesy. Prophetic gifts cannot be turned on at will – we can seek revelation but whether or not we receive is always God's prerogative. It is, however, possible that God is speaking to us more often than we realise, and training courses can help us become more attuned to whatever God may be saying to us concerning ourselves and others. Courses can help people significantly at the outset of their prophetic journey in the following ways:

### Courses encourage people to earnestly desire prophecy

Simply providing biblical and present-day examples of the often lifechanging effects of prophecy encourages people to pursue this gift. Some may be unaware that we can actively seek to prophesy, rather than it being something that 'just happens' passively. Being reminded that scripture encourages us to ask for the Holy Spirit and that God the Father wants to give us good gifts may seem basic but, if pursued, can have profound results.

As we are taught more about the nature of prophecy, putting what is learned into practice, we learn to become more attuned to the voice of the Spirit. And fears about extremism can be allayed once it is realised that prophecy is not a free-for-all, but that parameters and safeguards need to be in place.

For some, training courses act as encouragement to stir up the prophetic gift that is already within them (2 Timothy 1:6). It is easy to allow our gifts to lapse, either through busyness, laziness or discouragement. A training event or course can prompt us to leave the safe harbour of passivity and venture into the open sea.

## Courses help people to recognise the voice of God

Unless we become attuned to it, the voice of God can be difficult to recognise particularly if God speaks to us in unspectacular ways. Probably the clearest biblical example of this is of the young boy Samuel (1 Samuel 3). One night he heard a voice calling his name and assumed that he was being summoned by his mentor, Eli the priest. The more experienced Eli helped him realise who was actually seeking to attract his attention. He was helped to discern the voice of God.

I have a friend who sometimes asks me the unnerving question, 'What is God saying to you at the moment?' Despite feeling put on the spot, once I think about it, I can usually identify something that stands out. It may be that a verse of scripture has struck me. Sometimes there is a thought or a metaphor from the Bible that has been capturing my imagination for no discernible reason.

## We learn to create conditions that are conducive to prophecy

We are more likely to hear God when we are quiet, calm and focused. In 2 Kings 3:15, Elisha intentionally sought to create conditions conducive to his being able to discern the voice of the Lord. He did this by requesting a harpist to play for him. His mentor Elijah had heard God speak on Mount Horeb, but he had to listen hard since

God's voice took the form of an almost inaudible whisper. The whisper of God easily gets swamped by more spectacular and engrossing sights, the earthquake, wind and fire of 1 Kings 19:12.

The Elijah story is interesting. Even though God himself produced phenomenal sights and sounds he was not 'in' them (it might be easy for us to equate volume with God's presence). One rabbinic commentary on this particular passage describes the sound Elijah heard as the 'daughter of a voice'. This was in the days when, stereotypically, sons were boisterous, whereas daughters were much quieter. While we might feel this is an unenlightened, rather sexist concept, the point is that God's voice is not always the strongest and loudest voice we hear.

When we are distracted by other competing voices God's voice easily fades, unobtrusively, into the background. We are distractible and can easily miss God unless we deliberately develop ways to become attentive.

## We become aware of the evangelistic potential of prophecy

Gifts such as prophecy, words of knowledge, dreams and visions are not simply for the benefit of God's people. They are also the means by which God can communicate his love to those around us, even to those who are strangers to us. Like many Christians, I have had the experience myself of meeting a stranger and being given words to say which clearly hit the nail on the head. This can occur suddenly and come unbidden or it can be the result of our silently praying for the right words to say to someone.

So-called treasure hunting takes this principle a step further in what is termed 'prophetic evangelism'. For those involved in evangelism, this involves seeking and receiving guidance beforehand concerning people yet to be encountered on the streets or in other public areas. There is the expectation that God will reveal clues to those concerned as to the identity of specific people to be approached as well as particular needs for prayer, such as any physical ailments.

## Evaluating Aspects of Training

Some methods employed in prophetic training need careful evaluation and reconsideration. Such methods include: being encouraged to use objects visible in the vicinity, such as a painting or perhaps an item of furniture, as a spur and focus to stimulate prophecy; practising prophesying to others in pairs; as well as the aforementioned practice of 'treasure hunting'.

## Using what is seen to stimulate prophecy

Jeremiah 1 is used as the biblical justification for this practice. When asked by God what he saw, Jeremiah replied that he could see an almond branch and a boiling pot. God used the objects selected as metaphors to reveal his word to Jeremiah, although it is unclear whether Jeremiah saw actual physical objects or whether they were visions. Even if these were actual physical objects this example is, in fact, an exception, rather than being the means by which prophecy was commonly received.

I am not suggesting that this cannot happen today – I am sure it does and, in fact, only recently a painting in our home caught the attention of someone praying for me about a specific situation, and this gave rise to her subsequent prayer which turned out to be very prophetic in nature. If, however, we are encouraged as a matter of course to employ this practice, there is a lot of scope to (incorrectly) interpret what we see before us as being of prophetic significance. We should note that Jeremiah was asked *by God* 'what do you see?' It was not initiated by Jeremiah, nor was it the suggestion of another person and it was certainly not a technique designed to be used time and time again to stimulate prophecy.

## Working in pairs to prophesy to one another

Another commonly employed exercise is to divide people into pairs and encourage each person to say what is sensed about the other. At times, this can result in quite accurate prophetic words being given, but again there is room for error. This exercise also suggests that we can 'turn prophecy on' at will. I suspect that most often what happens is that the person 'prophesying' is enabled to get in touch more easily with their own inner world – or, with such active encouragement, is giving voice to subliminal clues about the other person.

There is rarely the opportunity in such exercises to reflect on particular words given and discern whether we are dealing with actual prophecy, subliminal clues or even making it up. The result of the overuse of this practice is that rather than a culture of discernment being created, prophecy is in danger of becoming devalued. In such instances, those participating may fail to employ the necessary skills for discernment, and a culture of 'anything goes' can result. Training courses can be used by God but only when critique and feedback are offered can they become true learning experiences.

If course attendees have the opportunity to operate prophetic gifts in the context of a Christian community or a local church, there is scope for the ongoing weighing of prophecy and for gifts to be gradually honed over time. When such a context is available, training exercises get people started and the ongoing involvement of more experienced people locally helps to refine prophetic practice. Where people engage in exercises without an ongoing context for local learning, quality control is limited, especially where discernment processes are lacking.

## Treasure hunting

Treasure hunting has received a lot of criticism and some people approached in public places have reported having received unwelcome attention. There are also reports bringing prophetic street evangelism into disrepute - for example, a group in the UK were told to offer to pray for back problems, since they are quite common! A friend who trained as an intern at Bethel Church, Redding, which advocates treasure hunting, told me that such criticism has been taken to heart. Processes have now been designed to ensure good, sensitive, practice with better quality control. In fact, many people have been reached in this way and I am not suggesting that this approach is actually invalid.

My main concern with this methodology is that it can, at times, represent a 'raiding party' approach to those outside the Church. We leave the security of the fort to venture forth 'into the wilds' around us and then return with our spoils back to the safety of the fort. As such, it may represent an alternative to the Church being truly incarnational.

The example of Jesus suggests that we should become embedded in our neighbourhood and workplace so that we make deep and meaningful connections with the people around us. Jesus 'became flesh and *dwelt* among us' and was well known in his local community, initially simply as a carpenter (John 1:14). Once we develop meaningful relationships with those around us, it may be that we no longer need quite as many words of knowledge as people will themselves tell us their needs and may even ask for prayer.

While 'treasure hunting' can and does co-exist alongside an incarnational approach, I am convinced that having an incarnational approach needs much greater emphasis in some circles. This requires people to make space in their lives for engagement with neighbours and with their local community more generally. For many, such an approach involves a major rethink as church life easily becomes all-consuming leaving little room for relationships with the unchurched. Although Jesus did receive revelation concerning individuals, it usually occurred in the course of meeting in the ordinary, everyday things of life (such as with Nathanael and the woman at the well).

My comments on treasure hunting perhaps present an overly negative picture since many people have encountered God's involvement in their lives through such means. My suggestion is that we place a higher value on time spent doing ordinary things with people outside the Church, not as a technique to get on to spiritual topics of conversation, but as a biblical way to live. If we really get to know people around us, experience suggests that we are more likely to be asked about the hope that is within us (1 Peter 3:15). We may even receive revelation to share with our friends, in normal, everyday settings and then be able to do so, in more natural ways, without having to create artificial contexts.

\* \* \* \* \* \*

Despite these reservations, I remain convinced that training courses can and do help us develop prophetic gifts, as long as insights and instructions given are imparted sensitively, allowing for variety of expression and outworking. The trap and temptation, both for those designing such courses and for attendees, is to fall back on prescribed techniques. Not only do one-size-fits-all approaches fail to capture the ingenuity and creativity of the ways in which God may speak to us, but also there is the danger that prophecy is actually rationalised and systematised in some way. *Learning to prophesy (and prophecy itself) must always be regarded as an art rather than a science.* Bearing these provisos in mind, courses also need to dovetail both with local church face-to-face involvement - and with our engagement in our local community - not to supplant real-life apprenticeship and learning.

## Untapped Resources for Growing in Prophecy

For several years, I have been involved in developing relationships between those in my own church circles (Non-denominational Charismatic Churches) and the Catholic Charismatic Renewal. This has been a fascinating voyage of discovery and has, for my part, shattered images of many previously held stereotypes.

One outcome has been the realisation that there is much to learn in other Christian traditions that can be of benefit to the particular understanding of prophecy that has developed in my own tradition. In particular, there exist tried and tested approaches to listening to God and to discerning the source of our thoughts and feelings, including the possibility that God might be speaking to us through our inner affections. In particular:

- Contemplation, practising silence and intentional listening create conditions conducive to awareness of what the Spirit might be saying. These practices, emphasised by so-called contemplative traditions of Christian spirituality, and until recently downplayed in evangelical circles, are now being rediscovered by Evangelicals and Charismatics alike.

- We have already mentioned that the process of distinguishing the voice of God from other voices can be helped by drawing on the rich resources of classical approaches to Christian spirituality. In particular, the principles for spiritual discernment utilised in Ignatian spirituality are underused in charismatic and evangelical circles.

Space does not permit more than a brief mention of the possibility that these deep and often untapped resources could be usefully explored by those interested either in growing themselves in the practice of prophecy or in developing others in the use of prophecy.[33]

---

[33] These practices are explored further in *Cultivating God's Presence: Renewing Ancient Practices for Today's Church.*

# 15

# REFRAMING PROPHECY TODAY

> Jesus needed to help his disciples to recognise a true and, as it happened, the greatest prophet - John the Baptist - in their midst and sometimes we too need help in discerning what and who is prophetic.
> SACRED SPACE (COMMENTING ON MATTHEW 17:10-13)

The central place of prophets and prophecy in the Bible is easily overlooked but they – and it – are everywhere to be seen. This fact is illustrated simply by listing those biblical prophets whose names begin with just one letter of the alphabet, the letter A. In the Old Testament, we have Abel (Luke 11:51), Abraham (Genesis 20:7), Ahijah (1 Kings 11:29), Asaph (2 Chronicles 29:30), Azzur (Jeremiah 28:1), and Amos.[34] The New Testament mentions Anna (Luke 2:36) and Agabus (Acts 21:10) so at least eight people whose names begin with A were regarded as being prophets, alongside many others including major biblical figures such as Moses and Elijah (Deuteronomy 18:15).

These biblical figures functioned in a whole variety of ways: some wrote down lengthy visions, some confronted Israel's leadership and yet others engendered hope, providing a way forward in seemingly hopeless situations. This paints a diverse picture but it exemplifies the importance prophecy and prophets played – and still play - in the life of God's people. If a century ago, you had suggested that prophecy would be an accepted part of the Christian scene, you may have been regarded as somewhat deluded. This has changed with the advent of

---

[34] Asaph is referred to as a 'seer' which is another term for a prophet, meaning one who sees.

the Pentecostal and Charismatic Movements, and, with the widespread acceptance of the gifts of the Spirit, prophecy has flourished.

The central place that the Holy Spirit plays in the life of the Church as a whole has been largely rediscovered and Christianity has been reframed, rightly in my opinion, as a religion with revelation, including that of prophecy, at its core. There is now the expectation that God might speak through ordinary people exercising prophetic gifts. Though not universally accepted, the idea that we can receive revelation directly from God is now mainstream. Prophecy is back, rehabilitated as a legitimate component of Christian life, in keeping with the witness of scripture.

Alongside these positive developments, there is also the need to re-evaluate how prophecy functions today in light of the testimony of the Old and New Testaments and of church history. This is a process of reframing the nature of prophecy and its place in the life of the Church. I am not an artist, but I am aware that a new frame changes how we perceive a painting. It helps us to see the same thing in a different way, accentuating certain parts which may have been overlooked before and minimising others which may previously have dominated. A new frame can enhance and even bring to life a painting which we might otherwise have walked past.

In order to take a fresh look at prophecy it has been necessary to seriously consider the nature of revelation. While some of this process has affirmed previously held views, there are also challenges to current practice that arise when the form and content of biblical prophecy are compared with that of contemporary prophecy. One example, as previously mentioned, concerns how biblical prophecy often involved the use of poetic language and imagery, whereas in certain arenas this can be virtually lacking in many prophecies given today.

In addition, the process of reframing prophecy can help us develop a more healthy relationship with gifts of revelation. Acknowledging the mix of human and divine elements in a prophecy can free us from having either to accept without question or reject something that is shared. An awareness that not every image formed in our minds is a vision, but that some are, can enable us to take a step back and to benefit both from people's own ideas and from revelation from God. The realisation that 'mistaken' prophecies do not mean that someone is a false prophet releases us from the pressure of needing to be seen to be right and fosters an openness to having our contributions weighed. Reframing prophecy can help us evaluate today's wider issues in prophecy, including some that are contentious.

## Hot Topics in Prophecy Today

Many positive advances have been made in the recovery of prophecy but we have also witnessed imbalances and excesses - weeds have grown up with the wheat. The exercise of discernment has *not* always been in evidence and several issues could be described as hot topics which divide Charismatic Christians. I want, very briefly, to look at two of these topics, outlining some principles that can help us as we attempt to evaluate these areas of charismatic life. These are purely illustrative of a methodology that can be used to critique several currently held views and current issues around prophecy.

### Issue 1: The idea that prophets are strategists

In some quarters, there is the understanding that prophets are primarily strategists who work alongside entrepreneurial leaders, who themselves are regarded as apostles. This view has been promoted against the backdrop of the Church's decline in the West. On the positive side, it identifies the fact that some leaders are indeed entrepreneurial and that such leaders are needed today. It also affirms the need for entrepreneurs to work in teams and to be in partnership with those, sometimes identified as being prophets, who ask probing questions and who can suggest creative ways forward.

How then do we evaluate such a claim? Perhaps the first test is to ask whether this represents the primary way in which prophets and prophecy operate in the Bible.

**1. Does this view represent the core of prophetic ministry as illustrated in scripture?**

As this view usually goes hand in hand with thoughts that apostles are entrepreneurs, we will first examine this particular claim. With regard to apostolic ministry recorded in the New Testament, we might well view Paul as being an entrepreneurial apostle. He did travel extensively and founded churches, but his letters reveal an emphasis on maintaining the relational integrity of his churches, on right belief resulting in right action, as well as the importance of the unity of all believers - none of which particularly sound like the burden of an entrepreneur. When it comes to the Apostle John we see something even further removed from a model of apostleship associated with innovation or organisational development. Rather John stressed the centrality of our relationship with God and our love for one another, which is far from the concerns of most entrepreneurs.

Although there are some examples in scripture of prophets who outlined strategy, this is not representative of what we typically see. When we do see a prophetic strategy in action it tends towards the highly unusual, such as the command to defeat the city of Jericho by marching around it or the need to delay a battle until the sound of marching feet is heard in the trees (2 Chronicles 5:24). This would hardly be likely to satisfy someone looking for sound strategy today and it certainly does not address issues of organisational development.

We do, however, see some examples in scripture where prophecy initiated and facilitated the release of a new push forward for the people of God. In the Old Testament, there was Haggai whose prophetic input was crucial to the construction of the temple in Jerusalem. In the New Testament, we see the prophetic word releasing Paul and Barnabas into their wider ministry (Acts 13:1-3). So a balanced view of scripture would suggest that although prophecy and prophets may sometimes provide strategic input this is not the usual way in which they functioned. To view all prophets as strategists is like basing our view of what dogs are like on the characteristics of Alsatians alone.

The second test that can be applied in evaluating such views is whether or not we see them illustrated throughout the history of the Church.

## 2. What can we learn from the Church through the ages?

There are examples in church history of prophetic input that was, in fact, highly strategic, as evidenced by George Fox who had a revelation concerning which places would be receptive to the gospel. A more recent example is that of Dennis Balcombe's call to become a missionary. He was at a church in Los Angeles when a woman began to speak in tongues. As it happened there was a Hebrew speaker in the congregation at the time who confirmed not only that she was speaking in fluent Hebrew but also that the interpretation - that Balcombe would be a missionary to China - was correct. In 1969, Balcombe received a subsequent prophecy directing him to base himself in Hong Kong. His extensive ministry and wide influence on the Chinese house churches are outlined in David Aikman's excellent book *Jesus in Beijing*.

Readers may be aware that little mention has been made of the so-called Kansas City Prophets. These figures, regarded by some as controversial, have been described elsewhere, by David Pytches and R T Kendall, for example. However, it transpires that some of their prophetic words have come to pass and have been well-documented, such as the prediction that the ministry of Mike Bickle's church would have a major impact on the Far East. Such prophecies, tried and tested to be accurate, exist alongside others which have yet to pass the test of time.

These examples could well be considered to be revelations concerning God's strategic purposes. Yet, in most cases, they rarely conform to the kind of input we might expect from most strategists since the details of the proposed 'strategies' are sparse. The view that prophets are strategists is relatively recent but has become 'orthodox' for some even though it represents a narrow understanding of the scope of prophecy. It may partly have come about because of the need to contextualise biblical terms such as prophets and prophecy to make them more accessible and understandable. It is based on a business model of church life and organisational theory and draws on a selective sample of prophecy in the Bible and church history. Although some prophecy may indeed be concerned with what might loosely be described as strategy, the model of the prophet as strategist is not representative of most prophetic ministry we see exercised in scripture.

## Issue 2: Prophecy & politics

This second topic has been stimulated by recent misguided political prophecies in the USA. The question here is not so much whether they were accurate (they weren't) but whether such prophecies are in themselves legitimate. The interface between prophecy and politics is a complex issue that could easily fill a whole book. The aim here is more limited: to briefly evaluate the issue of whether or not secular politics is a usual topic for prophecy, using the two questions asked in the previous section.

### 1. Does this view represent the core of prophetic ministry as illustrated in scripture?

We see in scripture that there was a clear role for prophetic ministry in what would now be referred to as 'the political arena' in ancient Israel. This role was especially critical at times when rulers and those in authority needed to hear the word of God as a corrective to their ideas or policies. *The most common form of prophetic intervention was that of confrontation* and there was no cosying up to those in power. Delivering prophecy clearly involved great risk, as is evident in the example of Nathan the prophet uncovering the nature of King David's sin.

The majority of prophecies came from those on the margins, not from the centre of power. In fact, the commonly used phrase 'speaking truth to power' best sums up the majority of political prophecies seen in the Bible. *It usually involved personal risk* as those prophesying were in a position of relative weakness and, having no official status, they had no privileged immunity from reprisals, nor did they have personal political power.

Particularly in the Old Testament, some prophecies were directed towards specific nations and rulers at that time. We need to bear in mind, however, that many of these oracles were *primarily intended to encourage Israel*. With some exceptions, such as that of Jonah, the majority of these prophecies were probably not delivered to the nations concerned. However, most Old Testament prophecies were not political in the popular sense of the term. Their focus was usually elsewhere, often related to two issues that involved both rulers and the general populace: *they highlighted the need for social justice and called Israel to live in the light of the holiness of God*. When it comes to the New Testament we see continuity with the Old Testament – Jesus speaks truth to power – but also discontinuity as the context for God's people is no longer that of a specific geographical area.

We might similarly ask how prophecy and politics were related in the ministry of Paul. He was commissioned to carry God's name 'before the Gentiles and *kings* and the children of Israel' (Acts 9:15). This played out in the latter chapters of Acts where he stands before the Sanhedrin, Felix the governor of Judea, Agrippa and Festus. In these instances, he was not only making a defence for his actions, but he was also proclaiming that Jesus had inaugurated a new Kingdom. Paul was speaking truth to power.

We also need to bear in mind the possibility of so-called *category errors*, where we assume two different things are actually one and the same. We should not confuse prophecy in ancient Israel, a theocracy, with prophecy in our own political setting, a secular democracy. The two simply do not equate. We cannot, for example, take the promise 'if my people who are called by my name humble themselves, and pray and seek my face and turn from their wicked ways, then I will hear from heaven and will forgive their sin and heal their land' and automatically apply it to a modern nation-state (2 Chronicles 7:14). This was a promise given to ancient Israel in the context of the dedication of a place of worship. It was also written at a time when the existence of God's people and the Land were intertwined, almost inseparable concepts. We do, of course, believe in praying for our nation but this scripture is not a carte blanche promise that was given to the UK or the USA or anywhere else and we cannot 'claim it' without using it out of context.[35]

If we somehow equate our nation with that of Israel, believing that we have a similar covenantal relationship, then our approach to prophecy is called into question. It is also of note that in New Testament times the Church was concerned with the state but only in terms of how its rule affected the ability of Christians to go about their lives as followers of God (1 Timothy 2:2).

## 2. What can we learn from the Church through the ages?

Interestingly, we do not see the Church seeking to influence the political arena until after the conversion of Constantine in the early 4th century. In the Middle Ages, Church and state were seen as being intertwined, whether that was the Catholic, Eastern Orthodox or the

---

[35] That is not to deny that at any specific point in time, this scripture might come into focus for a particular nation and, under God's hand, be of utmost relevance.

later Protestant Churches. The main exception to this concerned were marginalised churches, such as the Anabaptists.

Perhaps the most shining example of Christians directly engaging with politics in recent years is that of Dr Martin Luther King Jr. He took his inspiration from the prophets of the Old Testament, particularly from Amos, and he certainly spoke truth to power. He also described a call that seemed to resonate with that of Isaiah and Jeremiah and he extensively used the sort of poetic imagery and language that is characteristic of prophecy.

Other examples of Christians engaging politically with social issues are numerous. Those of us in the UK might look back to William Wilberforce and his associates who fought tirelessly for the abolition of slavery, despite much opposition and public scorn. We should note, however, that these examples demonstrate risk and personal involvement with the political process as well as being a lifetime's work and calling. They were not making prophetic predictions from positions of relative security without the real life engagement necessary in speaking truth to power.

Perhaps the final consideration in evaluating political prophecy is to be aware of the rise of nationalism, a belief that one's nation occupies a privileged place on the international stage. Patriotism is somewhat different as it describes affection for and devotion to our country, whereas nationalism, in the words of George Orwell, places one's nation 'beyond good and evil and [recognises] no other duty than that of advancing its interests'. This is a matter for the exercise of discernment as nationalism has been embraced by some churches in the past and is an ever-present temptation. It inevitably erodes discipleship, as we cannot serve two masters, God and nationalism. We also need discernment to recognise when nationalism is operative in the Church though disguised as patriotism.

Taking the biblical and historical evidence together it would appear that there are certain issues we should be aware of when we seek to evaluate a prophecy relating to politics. Among other issues raised by this brief review of the material we could ask:

- Is this prophecy speaking truth to power?

- Is the prophet at risk or is it delivered from a position of security?

- Does it confuse ancient Israel/the Church with my own nation?
- Is the Kingdom of God, the gospel, the main consideration (as with Paul) or is it more nationalistic?
- Does it express the main burden of the prophets, God's holiness and social justice?

The approach to these two examples (relating prophecy to what we find in scripture and church history) is suggested as a way to critique contemporary practice. It is especially important to recognise the historical context of any scriptures we use to justify particular views.

# 16

# Final Thoughts

At one point in his epic voyage Odysseus, the hero of Homer's *Odyssey*, had to traverse a narrow passage on either side of which lurked two monsters, Scylla and Charybdis, who preyed upon passing mariners. Fortunately, he did this successfully, though not without some cost in terms of his crew. Being 'between Scylla and Charybdis' has become an idiom for having to choose between two equally unacceptable alternatives. Navigating the tricky issues surrounding prophecy today is just such a dilemma. One alternative, an unacceptable one, is for us to dispense with prophecy altogether. We in the West are children of the Enlightenment, that period in history which elevated rationality above all else, when scientific methods were used to analyse problems, think of possible solutions and then test them in practice. The benefits of the Enlightenment have been immense in fields such as medicine and engineering.

As good Enlightenment offspring, however, we have applied these kinds of methodologies not just to science and the social sciences but to problems such as church decline in Europe and North America, although without any real improvement in the situation. We have rarely stopped to ask the necessary questions about why the early church actually grew exponentially. Instead, at times, especially in the 1990s with the development of the Church Growth Movement, we found ourselves applying principles of analysis, strategy and planning more appropriate to the business world than to the Church of Jesus Christ. Alongside this time-consuming and labour-intensive development, spiritual gifts were unwittingly relegated to a backseat position.

This is our Scylla, a many-headed monster that could devour us through overactivity and the inevitable disillusionment if the expected results are not forthcoming. Strategy and planning do, of course, have a vital role to play in *implementing* any direction we receive from God. We see this in, for example, Paul's missionary journeys which were planned so that the gospel could be taken to urban areas of high population density. This was highly strategic and fruitful in its results. Strategy has its place but *our real hope for the future is a rediscovery of the power of the Spirit and the central role that revelation is intended to play in the life of the Church.*

Strangely, it is Charismatics just as much as those in non-charismatic church circles who can lose sight of the Holy Spirit's leading and power. Miller and Yamamori, in their book *Global Pentecostalism*, describe how some Charismatic and Pentecostal churches have all but excluded spiritual gifts from their gatherings. Their work implies that some, for all intents and purposes, have ceased to be part of a movement and have now become routinised - even though the latest songs continue to be sung, worship allows no room for spontaneous contributions. This is one trap into which we can all too easily fall. The need to keep prophecy and other spiritual gifts central in church life, but to do so in a discerning way, was, in fact, the motivation for this book.

While Scylla was enormously dangerous, her rival, Charybdis, was even more formidable – a whirlpool capable of engulfing an entire ship, rather than simply consuming individuals one at a time. Perhaps Charybdis represents the other main challenge to the use of prophecy today – the disrepute into which it has been brought by poor practice and extremism.

In North America, a number of leading figures in the Christian world have recognised this danger and have signed a statement seeking to redress this situation.[36] While some of those involved in what might be considered poor practice are well-intentioned and many have apologised, there remains the need to gently confront excesses when they exist. The alternative is that the 'charismatic ship' is sucked under and we all go down with her, weighed down by criticism, both from within and outside the Church at large.

---

[36] https://propheticstandards.com

## The Silver and the Dross

> 'As silver is melted in a furnace...'
> EZEKIEL 22:22

I was initially encouraged to write a book on prophecy by Robb, a friend with very clear prophetic gifts, and someone who has been involved over the years in training others in prophecy. We had talked together about prophecy and words of knowledge and he felt that some of my reflections might help foster a wider discussion. I had considered the possibility of a book on prophecy before but had felt reticent. Not only is it a contentious subject with people holding divergent views but some of my conclusions might not be popular with my friends and acquaintances if my comments are felt to be unfair or misguided (which some may well be!).

Two weeks after I had started writing, I attended a conference in Rome. I took part in a small group to discuss the presentations we had heard and pray for one another. During a prayer time a young woman whom I had not met before shared what she believed to be a prophetic word for me. She was aware that I was writing a book on prophecy but had not been aware of my intended content. Her prophetic word was based on the previously quoted Ezekiel 22:22 which employs the image of a furnace refining silver.[37] In one sense this was an odd verse to share with me, as its original context was God's judgement on Israel. She was not suggesting the whole verse was relevant but rather emphasised the opening phrase - the description of a furnace removing impurities from silver ore.

A refining process results in the removal of impurities, the dross, as it rises to the surface and can be skimmed off to leave pure silver. This prophecy seemed to emphasise the understanding that the practice of prophecy in the charismatic wing of the Church is highly precious, as precious as silver, but that, as part and parcel of pure silver being produced, a refining process is needed to remove contaminants. I was not at all certain that I should attempt a critique of contemporary prophecy but I took this prophecy as an encouragement to proceed

---

[37] There was no suggestion that my writing would the fulfilment of this verse, nor that this was a new interpretation of Ezekiel 22:22. It was simply that Ezekiel's metaphor of a refining furnace was considered to be relevant to my writing.

despite feeling I might not make the best job of it. (I am reminded of G K Chesterton's aphorism: if a thing's worth doing, it is worth doing badly!)

I have attempted to avoid controversy and to establish some common ground although I realise that some of my suggestions are likely to cause disagreement. I regard my task as outlining certain ideas; the reader's task is to evaluate these suggestions and apply them in their particular context. Disagreement is not always a bad thing, at least it provides an opportunity to think through one's own position more clearly. Debate may even be a necessary component of the process by which we identify contaminating factors, allowing them to rise to the surface. My aim has been to help us engage with this process of separating the silver from the dross.

Fittingly perhaps, for me, a prophecy was an encouragement and confirmation that a book on prophecy should be written. Of course, even in my writing this material there needs to be a refining process and I hope that this book will encourage open conversations that will contribute to that end. For the most part, our thoughts on prophecy should be tentative, with suggestions for consideration, rather than firm conclusions. Redeeming Prophecy and it is not necessary to agree on every point before we can walk together and enjoy the unity to which we are called. Refining silver is a process conducted in several different ways, but perhaps for us, ongoing dialogue is a key element in refining our understanding and practice of prophecy.

When Paul wrote that 'the weapons of our warfare are not of the flesh' he was not referring to rebuking demonic powers, as is suggested by some. The strongholds he destroyed were the '*arguments and every lofty opinion* raised against the knowledge of God...' (2 Corinthians 10:4-5). We need to engage in dialogue even with those who think and operate in prophecy in very different ways from ourselves but we must engage with humility, recognising that we too hold views that may need adjustment or even correction.

Alongside engaging with and, at times, confronting poor prophetic practice we also need to continue to identify ways to promote *good* practice. Sometimes Charismatics undervalue the place of biblical studies in the understanding of our faith but knowledge, based on a firm understanding of scripture, can be hugely beneficial. Church history is another lens through which we can look and which reveals much as we try to evaluate prophecy today.

\* \* \* \* \* \*

Finally, I want to finish with both a statement and a question based on Isaiah 43:17-19:

> Remember not the former things,
> nor consider the things of old.
> Behold, I am doing a new thing;
> now it springs forth, do you not perceive it?

These verses follow a description of God's great saving act when the children of Israel were led through the waters of the Red Sea. Usually, when this is referred to in scripture it is to act as a reminder of God's power with the implication that we should look back and remember. Verse 18 is somewhat odd in that the prophet is telling his hearers to forget about it! His statement is essentially *don't look back*! We could apply this to the Charismatic and Pentecostal Movements today. Nostalgia is always a temptation particularly when we can look back to times when God has moved in spectacular and unusual ways.

Having told the people of Israel not to look back to former glorious days, Isaiah poses a fascinating question which we too do well to consider. He asked them what they saw God doing there and then. What 'new thing' do we perceive springing up? What we see God doing today won't be the same as that already seen and experienced before. It is a completely new and different thing, not an old thing, recycled or modified or improved slightly, but brand new and fresh, like new shoots of grass in the Spring.

It is likely that as each of us looks to see what God is doing now, what we see will be slightly different and will be represented in different ways. It is unlikely that we will see exactly the same thing. Our answers may be different, but it is an important, in fact, a vital question for us to consider. To answer that question requires seeing and looking, revelation and insight, spiritual perception and the Spirit of God. And these, of course, are the essential elements of prophecy. Prophecy helps us to see things differently; it literally reframes the way we see our world as God draws back the veil and reveals to us a new reality, the reality of his Kingdom breaking into our experience and the experience of those around us.

Thank you for reading Redeeming Prophecy, and for walking with me on this journey.

If you've found this book helpful, encouraging, or thought-provoking, I'd be deeply grateful if you could take a moment to leave a short review on Amazon or Goodreads. Reviews make a real difference - they help others discover the book and join the conversation.

You can scan the QR code below to leave a review on Amazon:

# Further Reading

## Prophecy Today

Bickle, M., Growing in the Prophetic. Lake Mary FL, Charisma House, 2008.

Cartledge M, 'Charismatic Prophecy'. *The Journal of Pentecostal Theology*, 5, 1994, pp.79-120.

Clark, R., & Healy, M., The Spiritual Gifts Handbook. Bloomington, Chosen Books, 2018.

Cooke, G., Developing Your Prophetic Gift. Lancaster, Sovereign World, 1994.

Deere, J., Surprised by the Voice of God. Grand Rapids, Zondervan, 1998.

Kendall, R.T., Prophetic Integrity. Nashville, Thomas Nelson, 2022.

Pytches, D., Some Said It Thundered. London, Hodder & Stoughton, 1990.

Talbot, J.M. & Rabey, S., Exploring the Gifts of the Spirit. Nashville, Thomas Nelson, 2020.

Whitehead, C., Towards a Fuller Life in the Holy Spirit. Luton, New Life, 2011.

Yocum, B., prophecy: Exercising the Prophetic Gifts of the Spirit in the Church. Ann Arbor, Servant Books, 1993.

## Spiritual Gifts in Church History

Cohn, N., The Pursuit of the Millennium. London, Paladin, 1970.

Harrell, D., All Things Are Possible. Bloomington, Indiana University Press, 1978.

Hyatt, E., 2000 Years of Charismatic Christianity. Lake Mary FL, Charisma House, 2002.

Penney, N., (ed), The Journal of George Fox. New York, Cosimo Classics 2007.

Olden, T., The Confession of St Patrick. Dublin, CrossReach Publications, 2016.

Synan, V., An Eyewitness Remembers the Century of the Holy Spirit. Grand Rapids, Chosen Books, 2010.

Turner, M., The Holy Spirit and Spiritual Gifts: Then and Now. Carlisle, Paternoster Press, 1996.

## Biblical Prophecy & Related Topics

Bauckham, R., The Theology of the Book of Revelation. Cambridge, Cambridge University Press, 1993.

Brueggemann, W., Hopeful Imagination: Prophetic Voices in Exile. Minneapolis, Fortress Press, 1978.

Brueggemann, W., The Prophetic Imagination. Minneapolis, Fortress Press, 1986.

Heschel, A., The Prophets, vol. i. New York: Harper and Row, 1962.

Heschel, A., The Prophets, vol. ii. New York: Harper and Row, 1962.

Hill, D., New Testament Prophecy. London, Marshall, Morgan and Scott, 1979.

Morris, L., Apocalyptic, Exeter, Paternoster Press, 1972.

Penney, J., 'The Testing of New Testament Prophecy'. *Journal of Pentecostal Theology*, 10, 1997, pp.35-84.

Prevost J, How to Read the Prophets. London, SCM, 1995, pp.1-39.

Von Rad, G., Old Testament Theology, vol. ii. London: SCM, 1965 (trans.), pp.1-119, 220-37, 319-37.

## The Context of the Early Church

Gehring, R., House Church and Mission: The Importance of Household Structures in Early Christianity. Peabody, MA, Hendrickson, 2004.

Malherbe, A., Social Aspects of Early Christianity. Philadelphia, Fortress, 1983.

Meeks, W., The First Urban Christians: The Social World of the Apostle Paul. New Haven, Yale University Press, 2003.

Rowlands, C., Christian Origins: An Account of the Setting and Character of the Most Important Messianic sect of Judaism. London, SPCK, 1985.

Young, F. and Ford, D., Meaning and Truth in 2 Corinthians. London, SPCK, 1987.

## Other Books Cited & Background Reading

Bartlett, R. S., 'Let Justice Roll Down Like Waters: The Model of Hebrew Prophecy in the Ministry of Martin Luther King, Jr.' *The Journal of the Interdenominational Theological Centre*, 21, 1993-4, pp.10-38.

Bauckham, R., Gospel of Glory: Major Themes in Johannine Theology. Grand Rapids, Baker Academic, 2015.

Brown, C., Article on 'Prophet'. *New International Dictionary of New Testament Theology.* Exeter, Paternoster Press, 1978, pp.74-89.

Brueggemann, W., 'The Prophet as a Destabilising Presence'. In Shelp, E., and Sunderland, R., (eds.) The Pastor as Prophet. New York, The Pilgrim Press, 1985, pp.49-77.

Geivett, R. and Pivec, H., A New Apostolic Reformation? A Biblical Response to a Worldwide Movement. Bellingham WA, Lexham Press, 2014.

Hocken, P., The Challenges of the Pentecostal, Charismatic and Messianic Jewish Movements: The Tensions of the Spirit. Farnham, Ashgate, 2009.

Lischer, R., Martin Luther King, Jr: Performing the Scripture. *Anglican Theological Review*, 77:2, 1995, pp.160-172.

McKnight, S., The Kingdom Conspiracy. Michigan, Brazos Press, 2014.

Miller, D. and Yamamori, T., Global Pentecostalism: The New Face of Christian Social Involvement. Berkley, University of California Press, 2007.

Overholt, T. W., Channels of Prophecy: The Social Dynamics of Prophetic Activity. Minneapolis, Fortress Press, 1989.

Peterson, J., Twelve Rules for Life. London, Penguin, 2018.

Ramsay, W. M., Four Modern Prophets. Atlanta, John Knox Press, 1986, pp.1-50, 89-96.

Roberts, R., Cultivating God's Presence: Renewing Ancient Practices for Today's Church. Beaminster, Finnian Press, 2020.

Roberts, R., The Characteristics of the New Charismatic Churches. http://www.christianunity.va/content/unitacristiani/en/dialoghi/sezione-occidentale/pentecostali/conversazioni-con-le-nuove-chiese-carismatiche/the-characteristics-of-the-new-Charismatic-churches.html

# About the Author

Dr Richard Roberts has spent four decades in leadership within New Charismatic Churches. He has taught widely and served as Director of Studies for a Master's degree in Missional Leadership, equipping church leaders for ministry in today's changing world. He was a trustee of Ffald y Brenin Retreat Centre in Wales.

Richard also serves on the organising committee for the Gathering in the Holy Spirit conference in Rome and has participated in official contact between the New Charismatic Churches and the Vatican.

He is the author of several books:

- *Rediscovering Church as Networks: The Ongoing Story of the New Charismatic Churches*
- *Saint Patrick: Resilience & Adaptability in Church Leadership*
- *Cultivating God's Presence: Renewing Ancient Practices for Today's Church*

Amazon author page:
https://www.amazon.co.uk/stores/author/B08X24N1X1

email: finnianpress@icloud.com

# SAINT PATRICK
*Resilience and Adaptability
in Church Leadership*

St Patrick's inspiring story invites us to consider a kind of leadership that comes from vulnerability, displacement, and dependence on God. Instead of clinging to power or status, Patrick relied on prayer and openness to the Spirit, and gained the courage to step into unknown territory.

---

*'In the ever-shifting landscape of contemporary Christian leadership, the journey of leading a church, home group, or any Christian organisation demands an inspired approach. Dr Richard J Roberts takes us on a transformative exploration, inviting us to learn insights from the resilient leadership of one of the most iconic figures in the history of the Church'*
Dr Gordon Robertson
Christian Broadcasting Network

---

These observations from Patrick's life prompt reflection on contemporary church leadership. *Saint Patrick* is a thoughtful resource for navigating challenges and finding inspirations amid the change which we too must learn to navigate.

# CULTIVATING GOD'S PRESENCE
*Renewing Ancient Practices for Today's Church*

Written for those who long to deepen their life with God, this book offers renewed patterns and rhythms for daily living that nurture God's presence.

---

*'Stand at the crossroads and look; ask for the ancient paths, ask where the good way is, and walk in it, and you will find rest for your souls. This is a book that will help pilgrims who are hungry for the Presence of God do just that. There are few books that when I read, I don't want to put down, fewer still that when I have read, I want to read all over again. This is one such book.'*
Anne de Leyser
Local Houses of Prayer (Ffald y Brenin)

---

Drawing inspiration from the Celtic monastic tradition, Richard Roberts weaves together historical example, personal experience, and biblical insight to offer a fresh, integrated approach to Christian discipleship for the twenty-first century.

Made in the USA
Monee, IL
03 May 2026